GreatBooks
Roundtable

Level 2

GreatBooks
Roundtable

Level 2

GreatBooks
Foundation

First Printing
4 6 8 9 7 5
Printed in the United States of America

Library of Congress Cataloging-in-Publication Data

Great books roundtable. Level 2.
   p. cm.
   ISBN 978-1-933147-54-3 (alk. paper)
   1. Reading (Middle school)–United States. 2. Reading comprehension–
United States. 3. Children–Books and reading–United States. I. Great
Books Foundation (U.S.)
LB1632.G74 2010b
372.47–dc22

                                       2009027260

Published and distributed by

THE GREAT BOOKS FOUNDATION
A nonprofit educational organization

35 East Wacker Drive, Suite 400

Chicago, IL 60601

www.greatbooks.org

CONTENTS

PREFACE

Welcome to Great Books Roundtable™! In this reading and discussion program, you will be using a learning method called **Shared Inquiry.**™ In Shared Inquiry, you develop your own **interpretation** of what you read.

Authors do not usually tell us exactly how the parts of a work of literature are connected or spell out why everything in a story happens.

But in good writing, everything fits together and is there for a reason. The parts of the text connect and support each other as the parts of a building do.

Because the parts of a good piece of writing are connected, they help explain one another. Good authors put into their writing the things a reader must know to understand what is happening and why. As you figure out for yourself why the things an author puts in a text are there, you are interpreting what you read. To **interpret** a text is to explain its meaning—what happens in it, and why, and what it is about. Many texts, like those in Great Books programs, support more than one interpretation. When you interpret a text, you are actively seeking out its meaning by asking and exploring questions.

HOW SHARED INQUIRY WORKS

In Shared Inquiry, you read literature that makes you **think and ask questions**.

After reading or listening to the story, poem, or essay, everyone in the group shares questions about it. Some questions can be answered right away. Others will be saved for discussion or other activities.

Everyone then rereads the text and makes notes. Afterward, you all compare your reactions to parts of the text.

You will develop your interpretation of a text most fully in **Shared Inquiry discussion**. During discussion, everyone thinks about the meaning of the text in depth. People sit so everyone can see all the members of the group, and the leader starts discussion with an **interpretive question**—a question that has more than one good answer that can be supported with evidence from the text.

What Shared Inquiry Discussion Looks Like

In a Shared Inquiry discussion, the leader isn't looking for the "right answer." Rather, the leader starts with a question that has more than one good answer based on the text and wants to hear ideas about it.

The leader asks questions to help everyone think more deeply.

In addition to sharing your ideas, you can agree or disagree with someone or ask him a question about his comment.

You can also ask someone to explain her idea a bit more.

At the end of discussion, people will have different answers to the opening question, but everyone will have a better understanding of the text and the evidence for his or her answer. You may change your answer because of what you hear in discussion or hear new evidence to support your original answer.

SHARED INQUIRY DISCUSSION:
FIVE GUIDELINES

People of all ages, from kindergartners to adults, participate in Shared Inquiry discussion groups. All participants follow these five guidelines, which help everyone share ideas about the text and learn from one another.

Read the text twice before participating in the discussion.

Discuss only the text that everyone has read.

3 Support your ideas with evidence from the text.

4 Listen to other participants, respond to them directly, and ask them questions.

5 Expect the leader to only ask questions, rather than offer opinions or answers.

SHARED INQUIRY DISCUSSION ETIQUETTE

DO
Let other people
talk, and listen to
what they say.

DON'T
Talk over people
and keep others
from speaking.

DO
Speak up! You may
have an idea no one else
has thought of.

DON'T
Be afraid to
share your ideas.

DO

Be willing to think
about new ideas.
Disagree politely.

DON'T

Take it personally
when someone disagrees
with your idea.

DO

Pay attention—it shows
respect for the members
of your group.

DON'T

Distract people or act
as if their ideas aren't
worth hearing.

TYPES OF QUESTIONS

Asking yourself questions is the most important thing you can do while you are reading. When you ask questions, you are helping yourself organize your thoughts about what in the text is interesting, confusing, surprising, shocking, funny, familiar, or sad. You are also preparing to explore the text more deeply the next time you read it. Below are different types of questions you might ask while reading. Notice that it's not always important—or even possible—to answer questions right away.

Factual questions can usually be answered after one thorough reading. The text provides information for a single correct answer.

EXAMPLES: *How old is the narrator when her mother starts going to work?* ("The White Umbrella")
Who is Diana Moon Glampers? ("Harrison Bergeron")
Why can't the narrator go to the school her mother wants her to go to? ("The First Day")

Background questions must be answered by information outside the text. They might be questions about the historical period in which the text is set, or questions about a character's culture. Sources that can help answer these questions include an encyclopedia, a textbook, the Internet, or a teacher who knows the subject.

EXAMPLES: *What is a boot camp?* ("The White Umbrella")
Where is La Cienega? ("El Diablo de La Cienega")
What happened during the Depression? ("The Cat and the Coffee Drinkers")

Evaluative questions go beyond the text and call for the reader's personal opinions. Such questions often ask for a judgment of events or a character's actions.

EXAMPLES: *Was it wrong for the narrator to accept the umbrella from Miss Crosman?* ("The White Umbrella")
Should the mother have tried harder to send the narrator to the first school? ("The First Day")
Should children be told about putting pets to sleep? ("The Cat and the Coffee Drinkers")

Speculative questions, like background questions, ask about information that exists outside the text, but readers must guess at or invent the answer using their imagination.

EXAMPLES: *Will the narrator continue to take piano lessons with Miss Crosman?* ("The White Umbrella")
Will Harrison's parents ever think about their son again? ("Harrison Bergeron")
Is the narrator going to be happy at her school? ("The First Day")

Interpretive questions, which get at the text's deeper meaning and themes, are the kind of questions that will be addressed in Shared Inquiry discussion. They have more than one good answer that can be supported with evidence from the text.

EXAMPLES: *Why does the narrator throw the white umbrella down a sewer?* ("The White Umbrella")
Why does Renate let Hanna try to cure her leg? ("Props for Faith")
Why does Miss Effie serve her students coffee? ("The Cat and the Coffee Drinkers")

READING STRATEGIES

Strong readers use certain strategies to help them understand what they read. If you are reading a confusing or puzzling passage, stop and try to figure out which of the reading strategies listed below might help you understand it more clearly. To help you keep track of which strategy you are using, mark your text in the margins with the letters or symbols suggested below:

R **REREADING** Go back and reread when you are reading something that is difficult to understand, or when you realize that you haven't been focusing on what you are reading.

? **ASKING QUESTIONS** Ask a question about something in the text you find puzzling or confusing.

C **MAKING CONNECTIONS** Connect or compare something that happens in the text with something you have experienced or learned yourself.

V **VISUALIZING** Create a picture in your head of what is going on in the text. Imagine sights, smells, sounds, and feelings.

! **NOTING STRONG REACTIONS** Stop and think about something in the text that causes you to feel a strong reaction (positive *or* negative).

I **MAKING INFERENCES** Combine clues in the text with your own ideas to fill in "missing pieces" of the text—places where the author doesn't directly tell you what's going on, but gives you hints by using description, dialogue, or other writing devices.

P **PREDICTING** Pause while reading and make a guess, based on your own ideas and the clues in the text, about what might happen next.

If you practice all these strategies, you will eventually begin to use several at a time automatically as you read. Using different comprehension strategies while reading, called *synthesizing*, is how a good reader comes to understand a complex text.

QUICK KEY to Marking Your Text	
R = Rereading	! = Noting strong reactions
? = Asking questions	I = Making inferences
C = Making connections	P = Predicting
V = Visualizing	

FOLLOW-UP QUESTIONS

In Shared Inquiry discussion, the leader isn't the only person who can ask questions. You can respond to your classmates directly by asking them questions yourself. These kinds of questions are called **follow-up questions** because they are useful to ask right after you hear an idea and want to find out more about it. Examples of follow-up questions include:

- Can you say more about what you mean?
- When you say the character is [word or phrase], what do you mean?
- When you say [word or phrase], what do you mean?
- What happened that gave you that idea?
- What part of the story supports your idea?
- What do you think about this other part?
- Are you agreeing with Emily's answer?
- Why do you agree with what Trevor said?
- So how does your idea fit with Walt's idea?

Remember: A follow-up question is a compliment. When you ask a follow-up question, you are showing that you are listening and thinking about what others are saying. When someone asks you a follow-up question, that person is displaying interest in your idea.

THE WHITE UMBRELLA

Gish Jen

When I was twelve, my mother went to work without telling me or my little sister.

"Not that we need the second income." The lilt of her accent drifted from the kitchen up to the top of the stairs, where Mona and I were listening.

"No," said my father, in a barely audible voice. "Not like the Lee family."

The Lees were the only other Chinese family in town. I remembered how sorry my parents had felt for Mrs. Lee when she started waitressing downtown the year before; and so when my mother began coming home late, I didn't say anything, and tried to keep Mona from saying anything either.

"But why shouldn't I?" she argued. "Lots of people's mothers work."

"Those are American people," I said.

"So what do you think we are? I can do the pledge of allegiance with my eyes closed."

Nevertheless, she tried to be discreet; and if my mother wasn't home by 5:30, we would start cooking by ourselves, to make sure dinner would be on time. Mona would wash the vegetables and put on the rice; I would chop.

For weeks we wondered what kind of work she was doing. I imagined that she was selling perfume, testing dessert recipes for the local newspaper. Or maybe she was working for the florist. Now that she had learned to drive, she might be delivering boxes of roses to people.

"I don't think so," said Mona as we walked to our piano lesson after school. "She would've hit something by now."

A gust of wind littered the street with leaves.

"Maybe we better hurry up," she went on, looking at the sky. "It's going to pour."

"But we're too early." Her lesson didn't begin until 4:00, mine until 4:30, so we usually tried to walk as slowly as we could. "And anyway, those aren't the kind of clouds that rain. Those are cumulus clouds."

We arrived out of breath and wet.

"Oh, you poor, poor dears," said old Miss Crosman. "Why don't you call me the next time it's like this out? If your mother won't drive you, I can come pick you up."

"No, that's okay," I answered. Mona wrung her hair out on Miss Crosman's rug. "We just couldn't get the roof of our car to close, is all. We took it to the beach last summer and got sand in the mechanism." I pronounced this last word carefully, as if the credibility of my lie depended on its middle syllable. "It's never been the same." I thought for a second. "It's a convertible."

"Well then make yourselves at home." She exchanged looks with Eugenie Roberts, whose lesson we were interrupting. Eugenie smiled good-naturedly. "The towels are in the closet across from the bathroom."

Huddling at the end of Miss Crosman's nine-foot leatherette couch, Mona and I watched Eugenie play. She was a grade ahead of me and, according to school rumor, had a boyfriend in high school. I believed it. Aside from her ballooning figure, she had auburn hair, blue eyes, and—I noted with a particular pang—a pure white folding umbrella.

"I can't see," whispered Mona.

"So clean your glasses."

"My glasses *are* clean. You're in the way."

I looked at her. "They look dirty to me."

"That's because *your* glasses are dirty."

Eugenie came bouncing to the end of her piece.

"Oh! Just stupendous!" Miss Crosman hugged her, then looked up as Eugenie's mother walked in. "Stupendous!" she said again. "Oh! Mrs. Roberts! Your daughter has a gift, a real gift. It's an honor to teach her."

Mrs. Roberts, radiant with pride, swept her daughter out of the room as if she were royalty, born to the piano bench. Watching the way Eugenie carried herself, I sat up, and concentrated so hard on sucking in my stomach that I did not realize until the Robertses were gone that Eugenie had left her umbrella. As Mona began to play, I jumped up and ran to the window, meaning to call to them—only to see their brake lights flash then fade at the stop sign at the corner. As if to allow them passage, the rain had let up; a quivering sun lit their way.

The umbrella glowed like a scepter on the blue carpet while Mona, slumping over the keyboard, managed to eke out a fair rendition of a catfight. At the end of the piece, Miss Crosman asked her to stand up.

"Stay right there," she said, then came back a minute later with a towel to cover the bench. "You must be cold," she

3

continued. "Shall I call your mother and have her bring over some dry clothes?"

"No," answered Mona. "She won't come because she . . ."

"She's too busy," I broke in from the back of the room.

"I see." Miss Crosman sighed and shook her head a little. "Your glasses are filthy, honey," she said to Mona. "Shall I clean them for you?"

Sisterly embarrassment seized me. Why hadn't Mona wiped her lenses when I told her to? As she resumed abuse of the piano, I stared at the umbrella. I wanted to open it, twirl it around by its slender silver handle; I wanted to dangle it from my wrist on the way to school the way the other girls did. I wondered what Miss Crosman would say if I offered to bring it to Eugenie at school tomorrow. She would be impressed with my consideration for others; Eugenie would be pleased to have it back; and I would have possession of the umbrella for an entire night. I looked at it again, toying with the idea of asking for one for Christmas. I knew, however, how my mother would react.

"Things," she would say. "What's the matter with a raincoat? All you want is things, just like an American."

Sitting down for my lesson, I was careful to keep the towel under me and sit up straight.

"I'll bet you can't see a thing either," said Miss Crosman, reaching for my glasses. "And you can relax, you poor dear. This isn't a boot camp."

When Miss Crosman finally allowed me to start playing I played extra well, as well as I possibly could. See, I told her with my fingers. You don't have to feel sorry for me.

"That was wonderful," said Miss Crosman. "Oh! Just wonderful."

An entire constellation rose in my heart.

"And guess what," I announced proudly. "I have a surprise for you."

Then I played a second piece for her, a much more difficult one that she had not assigned.

"Oh! That was stupendous," she said without hugging me. "Stupendous! You are a genius, young lady. If your mother had started you younger, you'd be playing like Eugenie Roberts by now!"

I looked at the keyboard, wishing that I had still a third, even more difficult piece to play for her. I wanted to tell her that I was the school spelling bee champion, that I wasn't ticklish, that I could do karate.

"My mother is a concert pianist," I said.

She looked at me for a long moment, then finally, without saying anything, hugged me. I didn't say anything about bringing the umbrella to Eugenie at school.

The steps were dry when Mona and I sat down to wait for my mother.

"Do you want to wait inside?" Miss Crosman looked anxiously at the sky.

"No," I said. "Our mother will be here any minute."

"In a while," said Mona.

"Any minute," I said again, even though my mother had been at least twenty minutes late every week since she started working.

According to the church clock across the street we had been waiting twenty-five minutes when Miss Crosman came out again.

"Shall I give you ladies a ride home?"

"No," I said. "Our mother is coming any minute."

"Shall I at least give her a call and remind her you're here? Maybe she forgot about you."

"I don't think she *forgot*," said Mona.

"Shall I give her a call anyway? Just to be safe?"

"I bet she already left," I said. "How could she forget about us?"

Miss Crosman went in to call.

"There's no answer," she said, coming back out.

"See, she's on her way," I said.

"Are you sure you wouldn't like to come in?"

"No," said Mona.

"Yes," I said. I pointed at my sister. "She meant yes too. She meant no, she wouldn't like to go in."

Miss Crosman looked at her watch. "It's 5:30 now, ladies. My pot roast will be coming out in fifteen minutes. Maybe you'd like to come in and have some then?"

"My mother's almost here," I said. "She's on her way."

We watched and watched the street. I tried to imagine what my mother was doing; I tried to imagine her writing messages in the sky, even though I knew she was afraid of planes. I watched as the branches of Miss Crosman's big willow tree started to sway; they had all been trimmed to exactly the same height off the ground, so that they looked beautiful, like hair in the wind.

It started to rain.

"Miss Crosman is coming out again," said Mona.

"Don't let her talk you into going inside," I whispered.

"Why not?"

"Because that would mean Mom isn't really coming any minute."

"But she isn't," said Mona. "She's *working*."

"Shhh! Miss Crosman is going to hear you."

"She's working! She's working! She's working!"

6

I put my hand over her mouth, but she licked it, and so I was wiping my hand on my wet dress when the front door opened.

"We're getting even *wetter*," said Mona right away. "Wetter and wetter."

"Shall we all go in?" Miss Crosman pulled Mona to her feet. "Before you young ladies catch pneumonia? You've been out here an hour already."

"We're *freezing*." Mona looked up at Miss Crosman. "Do you have any hot chocolate? We're going to catch *pneumonia*."

"I'm not going in," I said. "My mother's coming any minute."

"Come on," said Mona. "Use your *noggin*."

"Any minute."

"Come on, Mona," Miss Crosman opened the door. "Shall we get you inside first?"

"See you in the hospital," said Mona as she went in. "See you in the hospital with *pneumonia*."

I stared out into the empty street. The rain was pricking me all over; I was cold; I wanted to go inside. I wanted to be able to let myself go inside. If Miss Crosman came out again, I decided, I would go in.

She came out with a blanket and the white umbrella.

I could not believe that I was actually holding the umbrella, opening it. It sprang up by itself as if it were alive, as if that were what it wanted to do—as if it belonged in my hands, above my head. I stared up at the network of silver spokes, then spun the umbrella around and around and around. It was so clean and white that it seemed to glow, to illuminate everything around it.

"It's beautiful," I said.

Miss Crosman sat down next to me, on one end of the blanket. I moved the umbrella over so that it covered that too.

7

I could feel the rain on my left shoulder and shivered. She put her arm around me.

"You poor, poor dear."

I knew that I was in store for another bolt of sympathy, and braced myself by staring up into the umbrella.

"You know, I very much wanted to have children when I was younger," she continued.

"You did?"

She stared at me a minute. Her face looked dry and crusty, like day-old frosting.

"I did. But then I never got married."

I twirled the umbrella around again.

"This is the most beautiful umbrella I have ever seen," I said. "Ever, in my whole life."

"Do you have an umbrella?"

"No. But my mother's going to get me one just like this for Christmas."

"Is she? I tell you what. You don't have to wait until Christmas. You can have this one."

"But this one belongs to Eugenie Roberts," I protested. "I have to give it back to her tomorrow in school."

"Who told you it belongs to Eugenie? It's not Eugenie's. It's mine. And now I'm giving it to you, so it's yours."

"It is?"

She hugged me tighter. "That's right. It's all yours."

"It's mine?" I didn't know what to say. "Mine?" Suddenly I was jumping up and down in the rain. "It's beautiful! Oh! It's beautiful!" I laughed.

Miss Crosman laughed too, even though she was getting all wet.

"Thank you, Miss Crosman. Thank you very much. Thanks a zillion. It's beautiful. It's *stupendous*!"

"You're quite welcome," she said.

"Thank you," I said again, but that didn't seem like enough. Suddenly I knew just what she wanted to hear. "I wish you were my mother."

Right away I felt bad.

"You shouldn't say that," she said, but her face was opening into a huge smile as the lights of my mother's car cautiously turned the corner. I quickly collapsed the umbrella and put it up my skirt, holding onto it from the outside, through the material.

"Mona!" I shouted into the house. "Mona! Hurry up! Mom's here! I told you she was coming!"

Then I ran away from Miss Crosman, down to the curb. Mona came tearing up to my side as my mother neared the house. We both backed up a few feet, so that in case she went onto the curb, she wouldn't run us over.

"But why didn't you go inside with Mona?" my mother asked on the way home. She had taken off her own coat to put over me, and had the heat on high.

"She wasn't using her noggin," said Mona, next to me in the back seat.

"I should call next time," said my mother. "I just don't like to say where I am."

That was when she finally told us that she was working as a checkout clerk in the A&P. She was supposed to be on the day shift, but the other employees were unreliable, and her boss had promised her a promotion if she would stay until the evening shift filled in.

For a moment no one said anything. Even Mona seemed to find the revelation disappointing.

"A promotion already!" she said, finally.

I listened to the windshield wipers.

"You're so quiet." My mother looked at me in the rearview mirror. "What's the matter?"

"I wish you would quit," I said after a moment.

She sighed. "The Chinese have a saying: One beam cannot hold the roof up."

"But Eugenie Roberts's father supports their family."

She sighed once more. "Eugenie Roberts's father is Eugenie Roberts's father," she said.

As we entered the downtown area, Mona started leaning hard against me every time the car turned right, trying to push me over. Remembering what I had said to Miss Crosman, I tried to maneuver the umbrella under my leg so she wouldn't feel it.

"What's under your skirt?" Mona wanted to know as we came to a traffic light. My mother, watching us in the rearview mirror again, rolled slowly to a stop.

"What's the matter?" she asked.

"There's something under her skirt?" said Mona, pulling at me. "Under her skirt?"

Meanwhile, a man crossing the street started to yell at us. "Who do you think you are, lady?" he said. "You're blocking the whole damn crosswalk."

We all froze. Other people walking by stopped to watch.

"Didn't you hear me?" he went on, starting to thump on the hood with his fist. "Don't you speak English?"

My mother began to back up, but the car behind us honked. Luckily, the light turned green right after that. She sighed in relief.

"What were you saying, Mona?" she asked.

We wouldn't have hit the car behind us that hard if he hadn't been moving too, but as it was our car bucked violently, throwing us all first back and then forward.

"Uh oh," said Mona when we stopped. *"Another* accident."

I was relieved to have attention diverted from the umbrella. Then I noticed my mother's head, tilted back onto the seat. Her eyes were closed.

"Mom!" I screamed. "Mom! Wake up!"

She opened her eyes. "Please don't yell," she said. "Enough people are going to yell already."

"I thought you were dead," I said, starting to cry. "I thought you were dead."

She turned around, looked at me intently, then put her hand to my forehead.

"Sick," she confirmed. "Some kind of sick is giving you crazy ideas."

As the man from the car behind us started tapping on the window, I moved the umbrella away from my leg. Then Mona and my mother were getting out of the car. I got out after them; and while everyone else was inspecting the damage we'd done, I threw the umbrella down a sewer.

HARRISON BERGERON

Kurt Vonnegut Jr.

The year was 2081, and everybody was finally equal. They weren't only equal before God and the law. They were equal every which way. Nobody was smarter than anybody else. Nobody was better-looking than anybody else. Nobody was stronger or quicker than anybody else. All this equality was due to the 211th, 212th, and 213th Amendments to the Constitution, and to the unceasing vigilance of agents of the United States Handicapper General.

Some things about living still weren't quite right, though. April, for instance, still drove people crazy by not being springtime. And it was in that clammy month that the H-G men took George and Hazel Bergeron's fourteen-year-old son, Harrison, away.

It was tragic, all right, but George and Hazel couldn't think about it very hard. Hazel had a perfectly average intelligence, which meant she couldn't think about anything except in short bursts. And George, while his intelligence was way above normal, had a little mental handicap radio in his ear. He was required by law to wear it at all times. It was tuned to a government transmitter. Every twenty seconds or so, the transmitter would send out some sharp noise to keep people like George from taking unfair advantage of their brains.

George and Hazel were watching television. There were tears on Hazel's cheeks, but she'd forgotten for the moment what they were about.

On the television screen were ballerinas.

A buzzer sounded in George's head. His thoughts fled in panic, like bandits from a burglar alarm.

"That was a real pretty dance, that dance they just did," said Hazel.

"Huh?" said George.

"That dance—it was nice," said Hazel.

"Yup," said George. He tried to think a little about the ballerinas. They weren't really very good—no better than anybody else would have been, anyway. They were burdened with sash weights and bags of birdshot, and their faces were masked, so that no one, seeing a free and graceful gesture or a pretty face, would feel like something the cat drug in. George was toying with the vague notion that maybe dancers shouldn't be handicapped. But he didn't get very far with it before another noise in his ear radio scattered his thoughts.

George winced. So did two out of the eight ballerinas.

Hazel saw him wince. Having no mental handicap herself, she had to ask George what the latest sound had been.

"Sounded like somebody hitting a milk bottle with a ballpeen hammer," said George.

"I'd think it would be real interesting, hearing all the different sounds," said Hazel, a little envious. "All the things they think up."

"Um," said George.

"Only, if I was Handicapper General, you know what I would do?" said Hazel. Hazel, as a matter of fact, bore a strong resemblance to the Handicapper General, a woman named Diana Moon Glampers. "If I was Diana Moon Glampers," said Hazel, "I'd have chimes on Sunday—just chimes. Kind of in honor of religion."

"I could think, if it was just chimes," said George.

"Well—maybe make 'em real loud," said Hazel. "I think I'd make a good Handicapper General."

"Good as anybody else," said George.

"Who knows better'n I do what normal is?" said Hazel.

"Right," said George. He began to think glimmeringly about his abnormal son who was now in jail, about Harrison, but a twenty-one-gun salute in his head stopped that.

"Boy!" said Hazel, "that was a doozy, wasn't it?"

It was such a doozy that George was white and trembling, and tears stood on the rims of his red eyes. Two of the eight ballerinas had collapsed to the studio floor, were holding their temples.

"All of a sudden you look so tired," said Hazel. "Why don't you stretch out on the sofa, so's you can rest your handicap bag on the pillows, honeybunch." She was referring to the forty-seven pounds of birdshot in a canvas bag, which was padlocked around George's neck. "Go on and rest the bag for a little while," she said. "I don't care if you're not equal to me for a while."

George weighed the bag with his hands. "I don't mind it," he said. "I don't notice it anymore. It's just a part of me."

"You been so tired lately—kind of wore out," said Hazel. "If there was just some way we could make a little hole in the bottom of the bag, and just take out a few of them lead balls. Just a few."

"Two years in prison and two thousand dollars fine for every ball I took out," said George. "I don't call that a bargain."

"If you could just take a few out when you came home from work," said Hazel. "I mean—you don't compete with anybody around here. You just set around."

"If I tried to get away with it," said George, "then other people'd get away with it—and pretty soon we'd be right back to the dark ages again, with everybody competing against everybody else. You wouldn't like that, would you?"

"I'd hate it," said Hazel.

"There you are," said George. "The minute people start cheating on laws, what do you think happens to society?"

If Hazel hadn't been able to come up with an answer to this question, George couldn't have supplied one. A siren was going off in his head.

"Reckon it'd fall all apart," said Hazel.

"What would?" said George blankly.

"Society," said Hazel uncertainly. "Wasn't that what you just said?"

"Who knows?" said George.

The television program was suddenly interrupted for a news bulletin. It wasn't clear at first as to what the bulletin was about, since the announcer, like all announcers, had a serious speech impediment. For about half a minute, and in a state of high excitement, the announcer tried to say, "Ladies and gentlemen—"

He finally gave up, handed the bulletin to a ballerina to read.

"That's all right—" Hazel said of the announcer, "he tried. That's the big thing. He tried to do the best he could with what God gave him. He should get a nice raise for trying so hard."

"Ladies and gentlemen—" said the ballerina, reading the bulletin. She must have been extraordinarily beautiful, because the mask she wore was hideous. And it was easy to see that she was the strongest and most graceful of all the dancers, for her handicap bags were as big as those worn by two-hundred-pound men.

And she had to apologize at once for her voice, which was a very unfair voice for a woman to use. Her voice was a warm, luminous, timeless melody. "Excuse me—" she said, and she began again, making her voice absolutely uncompetitive.

"Harrison Bergeron, age fourteen," she said in a grackle squawk, "has just escaped from jail, where he was held on suspicion of plotting to overthrow the government. He is a genius and an athlete, is under-handicapped, and should be regarded as extremely dangerous."

A police photograph of Harrison Bergeron was flashed on the screen upside down, then sideways, upside down again, then right side up. The picture showed the full length of Harrison against a background calibrated in feet and inches. He was exactly seven feet tall.

The rest of Harrison's appearance was Halloween and hardware. Nobody had ever borne heavier handicaps. He had outgrown hindrances faster than the H-G men could think them up. Instead of a little ear radio for a mental handicap, he wore a tremendous pair of earphones, and spectacles with thick wavy lenses. The spectacles were intended to make him not only half blind, but to give him whanging headaches besides.

Scrap metal was hung all over him. Ordinarily, there was a certain symmetry, a military neatness to the handicaps issued to strong people, but Harrison looked like a walking junkyard. In the race of life, Harrison carried three hundred pounds.

And to offset his good looks, the H-G men required that he wear at all times a red rubber ball for a nose, keep his eyebrows shaved off, and cover his even white teeth with black caps at snaggle-tooth random.

"If you see this boy," said the ballerina, "do not—I repeat, do not—try to reason with him."

There was the shriek of a door being torn from its hinges.

Screams and barking cries of consternation came from the television set. The photograph of Harrison Bergeron on the screen jumped again and again, as though dancing to the tune of an earthquake.

George Bergeron correctly identified the earthquake, and well he might have—for many was the time his own home had danced to the same crashing tune. "My God—" said George, "that must be Harrison!"

The realization was blasted from his mind instantly by the sound of an automobile collision in his head.

When George could open his eyes again, the photograph of Harrison was gone. A living, breathing Harrison filled the screen.

Clanking, clownish, and huge, Harrison stood in the center of the studio. The knob of the uprooted studio door was still in his hand. Ballerinas, technicians, musicians, and announcers cowered on their knees before him, expecting to die.

"I am the Emperor!" cried Harrison. "Do you hear? I am the Emperor! Everybody must do what I say at once!" He stamped his foot and the studio shook.

"Even as I stand here—" he bellowed, "crippled, hobbled, sickened—I am a greater ruler than any man who ever lived! Now watch me become what I *can* become!"

Harrison tore the straps of his handicap harness like wet tissue paper, tore straps guaranteed to support five thousand pounds.

Harrison's scrap-iron handicaps crashed to the floor.

Harrison thrust his thumbs under the bar of the padlock that secured his head harness. The bar snapped like celery. Harrison smashed his headphones and spectacles against the wall.

He flung away his rubber-ball nose, revealed a man that would have awed Thor, the god of thunder.

"I shall now select my Empress!" he said, looking down on the cowering people. "Let the first woman who dares rise to her feet claim her mate and her throne!"

A moment passed, and then a ballerina arose, swaying like a willow.

Harrison plucked the mental handicap from her ear, snapped off her physical handicaps with marvelous delicacy. Last of all, he removed her mask.

She was blindingly beautiful.

"Now—" said Harrison, taking her hand, "shall we show the people the meaning of the word dance? Music!" he commanded.

The musicians scrambled back into their chairs, and Harrison stripped them of their handicaps, too. "Play your best," he told them, "and I'll make you barons and dukes and earls."

The music began. It was normal at first—cheap, silly, false. But Harrison snatched two musicians from their chairs, waved them like batons as he sang the music as he wanted it played. He slammed them back into their chairs.

The music began again and was much improved.

Harrison and his Empress merely listened to the music for a while—listened gravely, as though synchronizing their heartbeats with it.

They shifted their weight to their toes.

Harrison placed his big hands on the girl's tiny waist, letting her sense the weightlessness that would soon be hers.

And then, in an explosion of joy and grace, into the air they sprang!

Not only were the laws of the land abandoned, but the law of gravity and the laws of motion as well.

They reeled, whirled, swiveled, flounced, capered, gamboled, and spun.

They leaped like deer on the moon.

The studio ceiling was thirty feet high, but each leap brought the dancers nearer to it.

It became their obvious intention to kiss the ceiling.

They kissed it.

And then, neutralizing gravity with love and pure will, they remained suspended in air inches below the ceiling, and they kissed each other for a long, long time.

It was then that Diana Moon Glampers, the Handicapper General, came into the studio with a double-barreled ten-gauge shotgun. She fired twice, and the Emperor and the Empress were dead before they hit the floor.

Diana Moon Glampers loaded the gun again. She aimed it at the musicians and told them they had ten seconds to get their handicaps back on.

It was then that the Bergerons' television tube burned out.

Hazel turned to comment about the blackout to George. But George had gone out into the kitchen for a can of beer.

George came back in with the beer, paused while a handicap signal shook him up. And then he sat down again. "You been crying?" he said to Hazel.

"Yup," she said.

"What about?" he said.

"I forget," she said. "Something real sad on television."

"What was it?" he said.

"It's all kind of mixed up in my mind," said Hazel.

"Forget sad things," said George.

"I always do," said Hazel.

"That's my girl," said George. He winced. There was the sound of a riveting gun in his head.

"Gee—I could tell that one was a doozy," said Hazel.

"You can say that again," said George.

"Gee—" said Hazel, "I could tell that one was a doozy."

THE FIRST DAY

Edward P. Jones

On an otherwise unremarkable September morning, long before I learned to be ashamed of my mother, she takes my hand and we set off down New Jersey Avenue to begin my very first day of school. I am wearing a checkeredlike blue and green cotton dress, and scattered about these colors are bits of yellow and white and brown. My mother has uncharacteristically spent nearly an hour on my hair that morning, plaiting and replaiting so that now my scalp tingles. Whenever I turn my head quickly, my nose fills with the faint smell of Dixie Peach hair grease. The smell is somehow a soothing one now and I will reach for it time and time again before the morning ends. All the plaits, each with a blue barrette near the tip and each twisted into an uncommon sturdiness, will last until I go to bed that night, something that has never happened before. My stomach is full of milk and oatmeal sweetened with brown sugar. Like everything else I have on, my pale green slip and underwear are new, the underwear having come three to a plastic package with a little girl on the front who appears to be dancing. Behind my ears, my mother, to stop my whining, has dabbed the stingiest bit of her gardenia perfume, the last present my father gave her before he disappeared into memory. Because I cannot smell it, I have only her word that the perfume is there. I am also wearing yellow socks trimmed with thin lines of black and white around the tops. My shoes are my greatest joy, black patent leather miracles, and when one is nicked at the toe later that morning in class, my heart will break.

I am carrying a pencil, a pencil sharpener, and a small ten-cent tablet with a black-and-white speckled cover. My mother does not believe that a girl in kindergarten needs such things, so I am taking them only because of my insistent whining and because they are presents from our neighbors, Mary Keith and Blondelle Harris. Miss Mary and Miss Blondelle are watching my two younger sisters until my mother returns. The women are as precious to me as my mother and sisters. Out playing one day, I have overheard an older child, speaking to another child, call Miss Mary and Miss Blondelle a word that is brand new to me. This is my mother: When I say the word in fun to one of my sisters, my mother slaps me across the mouth and the word is lost for years and years.

All the way down New Jersey Avenue, the sidewalks are teeming with children. In my neighborhood, I have many friends, but I see none of them as my mother and I walk. We cross New York Avenue, we cross Pierce Street, and we cross L and K, and still I see no one who knows my name. At I Street, between New Jersey Avenue and Third Street, we enter Seaton Elementary School, a timeworn, sad-faced building across the street from my mother's church, Mt. Carmel Baptist.

Just inside the front door, women out of the advertisements in *Ebony* are greeting other parents and children. The woman who greets us has pearls thick as jumbo marbles that come

24

down almost to her navel, and she acts as if she had known me all my life, touching my shoulder, cupping her hand under my chin. She is enveloped in a perfume that I only know is not gardenia. When, in answer to her question, my mother tells her that we live at 1227 New Jersey Avenue, the woman first seems to be picturing in her head where we live. Then she shakes her head and says that we are at the wrong school, that we should be at Walker-Jones.

My mother shakes her head vigorously. "I want her to go here," my mother says. "If I'da wanted her someplace else, I'da took her there." The woman continues to act as if she has known me all my life, but she tells my mother that we live beyond the area that Seaton serves. My mother is not convinced and for several more minutes she questions the woman about why I cannot attend Seaton. For as many Sundays as I can remember, perhaps even Sundays when I was in her womb, my mother has pointed across I Street to Seaton as we come and go to Mt. Carmel. "You gonna go there and learn about the whole world." But one of the guardians of that place is saying no, and no again. I am learning this about my mother: The higher up on the scale of respectability a person is—and teachers are rather high up in her eyes—the less she is liable to let them push her around. But finally, I see in her eyes the closing gate, and she takes my hand and we leave the building. On the steps, she stops as people move past us on either side.

"Mama, I can't go to school?"

She says nothing at first, then takes my hand again and we are down the steps quickly and nearing New Jersey Avenue before I can blink. This is my mother: She says, "One monkey don't stop no show."

Walker-Jones is a larger, newer school and I immediately like it because of that. But it is not across the street from my mother's church, her rock, one of her connections to God, and I sense her doubts as she absently rubs her thumb over the back of her hand. We find our way to the crowded auditorium where gray metal chairs are set up in the middle of the room. Along the wall to the left are tables and other chairs. Every chair seems occupied by a child or adult. Somewhere in the room a child is crying, a cry that rises above the buzz-talk of so many people. Strewn about the floor are dozens and dozens of pieces of white paper, and people are walking over them without any thought of picking them up. And seeing this lack of concern, I am all of a sudden afraid.

"Is this where they register for school?" my mother asks a woman at one of the tables.

The woman looks up slowly as if she has heard this question once too often. She nods. She is tiny, almost as small as the girl standing beside her. The woman's hair is set in a mass of curlers and all of those curlers are made of paper money, here a dollar bill, there a five-dollar bill. The girl's hair is arrayed in curls, but some of them are beginning to droop and this makes me happy. On the table beside the woman's pocketbook is a large notebook, worthy of someone in high school, and looking at me looking at the notebook, the girl places her hand possessively on it. In her other hand she holds several pencils with thick crowns of additional erasers.

"These the forms you gotta use?" my mother asks the woman, picking up a few pieces of the paper from the table. "Is this what you have to fill out?"

The woman tells her yes, but that she need fill out only one.

"I see," my mother says, looking about the room. Then: "Would you help me with this form? That is, if you don't mind."

The woman asks my mother what she means.

"This form. Would you mind helpin me fill it out?"

The woman still seems not to understand.

"I can't read it. I don't know how to read or write, and I'm askin you to help me." My mother looks at me, then looks away. I know almost all of her looks, but this one is brand new to me. "Would you help me, then?"

The woman says Why sure, and suddenly she appears happier, so much more satisfied with everything. She finishes the form for her daughter and my mother and I step aside to wait for her. We find two chairs nearby and sit. My mother is now diseased, according to the girl's eyes, and until the moment her mother takes her and the form to the front of the auditorium, the girl never stops looking at my mother. I stare back at her. "Don't stare," my mother says to me. "You know better than that."

Another woman out of the *Ebony* ads takes the woman's child away. Now, the woman says upon returning, let's see what we can do for you two.

My mother answers the questions the woman reads off the form. They start with my last name, and then on to the first and middle names. This is school, I think. This is going to school. My mother slowly enunciates each word of my name. This is my mother: As the questions go on, she takes from her pocketbook document after document, as if they will support my right to attend school, as if she has been saving them up for just this moment. Indeed, she takes out more papers than I have ever seen her do in other places: my birth certificate, my baptismal record, a doctor's letter concerning my bout with chicken pox, rent receipts, records of immunization, a letter about our public assistance payments, even her marriage license—every single paper that has anything even remotely to do with my five-year-old life. Few of the papers are needed here, but it does not matter and my mother continues to pull out the documents with the purposefulness of a magician pulling out a long string of scarves. She has learned that money is the beginning and end of everything in this world, and when the woman finishes, my mother offers her fifty cents, and the woman accepts it without hesitation. My mother and I are just about the last parent and child in the room.

My mother presents the form to a woman sitting in front of the stage, and the woman looks at it and writes something on a white card, which she gives to my mother. Before long, the woman who has taken the girl with the drooping curls appears from behind us, speaks to the sitting woman, and introduces herself to my mother and me. She's to be my teacher, she tells my mother. My mother stares.

We go into the hall, where my mother kneels down to me. Her lips are quivering. "I'll be back to pick you up at twelve o'clock. I don't want you to go nowhere. You just wait right here. And listen to every word she say." I touch her lips and press them together. It is an old, old game between us. She puts my hand down at my side, which is not part of the game. She stands and looks a second at the teacher, then she turns and walks away. I see where she has darned one of her socks the night before. Her shoes make loud sounds in the hall. She passes through the doors and I can still hear the loud sounds of her shoes. And even when the teacher turns me toward the classrooms and I hear what must be the singing and talking of all the children in the world, I can still hear my mother's footsteps above it all.

PROPS FOR FAITH

Ursula Hegi

When our housekeeper told me she didn't think the midwife was Renate's real mother, I wondered if my best friend's parents were gypsies, those dark-haired women and men who, every July, set up the carnival on the Burgdorf fairgrounds and, with brown, ring-covered hands, took the groschen I'd saved for rides on the ferris wheel and pink clouds of cotton candy. *Gypsies.* That would explain Renate's dark, frizzy hair, her quick, black eyes. But gypsies moved rapidly, while my friend walked with a limp, her feet in patent leather shoes, her fragile ankles hidden under white knee socks that never stayed up.

Besides—gypsies were known to steal babies.

Not give them away.

After swearing me to secrecy, Frau Brocker told me, "I figure her real parents were too poor to keep her. Too many other children already." She'd just come back from her weekly visit to the beauty parlor and she smelled of hair spray. "Instead of paying the midwife, they must have given her the baby."

31

The midwife was a blond, heavy widow whose husband had been killed during the war on the Russian front. She'd delivered me and most of the kids I knew. Her name was Hilde Eberhardt, and she lived with her older son, Adi, and Renate in a white stucco house two blocks from school. No one had seen her pregnant with Renate, not even Trudi Montag. Twelve years before the midwife had left town one Thursday, and the following day she had returned with a dark-haired infant girl, claiming it was hers. By then her son had lived half of his five years without a father.

Renate didn't come to our school until the end of second grade, and we became best friends right away. Nearly two years earlier, she'd been taken to the Theresienheim with pneumonia. On the day she was to be released, she fell when she climbed out of bed, caved in on herself like a puppet whose strings had been cut. The nuns suspected polio and rushed her to St. Lukas Hospital in Düsseldorf where the doctors confirmed the diagnosis and kept her for over a year, probing her legs with needles. Though she was eventually cured, her left leg was shorter than the other. Thinner. Both legs were pale with large pores.

Whenever Renate took me to her house, the midwife examined the soles of our shoes and followed us around with a mop, catching any speck of dust that dropped from our skirts and settled on her glossy parquet floor. Yet, when I got ready to leave, she'd say, "Come back, Hanna. Any time."

Their yard, too, was orderly: a lush lawn without dandelions; window boxes with forget-me-nots and geraniums; a trimmed hedge of purple lilacs. The one imperfection was a pear tree that produced abundant blossoms but only yielded hard little pears with brown spots.

With his blond hair and blue eyes, Renate's brother, Adi, didn't look anything like Renate. His full name was Adolf, but no one called him that. Quite a few boys in the grades above us were called Adolf—a name that had been popular for babies born in the early war years—but we had no Adolfs in our class or in the younger grades. The name Adolf Hitler was never mentioned in our history classes. Our teachers dealt in detail with the old Greeks and Romans; we'd slowly wind our way up to Attila the Hun, to Henry the Eighth who had six wives, to Kaiser Wilhelm, to the First World War; from there we'd slide right back to the old Greeks and Romans.

In gym class Renate was always the last in line—awkward, hesitant, everything about her slow except for those dark eyes that seemed to move right through me. But I hardly thought about the polio or her leg until Sybille Immers, the butcher's daughter, called Renate a gimp one day as we left school. I leapt at Sybille, who was taller and heavier than I, kicking her shins; she raked her fingernails across my face and tore at my hair. When Frau Buttgereit, our music teacher, pulled us apart, her green hat with the pheasant feather fell into a puddle.

I still can't understand what I did less than a week later when Renate didn't want to come out and play.

"Why not?" I shouted, standing outside her bedroom window.

She leaned on the windowsill with both hands. "Because," she shouted back.

"Because why?"

"Because Sybille is coming over."

The scratches on my face still itched, and there she was, looking for a new best friend. Something hot and sad and mean rose inside me and, before I could stop myself, I yelled, "Even the gypsies didn't want to keep a gimp like you!"

Her arms tight against her body, Renate stood motionless. Her face turned red, then ashen.

I stared at her, horrified by what I had said. My throat ached, and when I tried to talk, I couldn't bring out one word.

"Hanna!" the side door slammed and the midwife ran toward me, her eyes filled with tears. "Don't you ever come back here," she shouted and raised one hand. "You hear me, Hanna?"

"But I didn't mean it," I cried out as I ran from her.

"I didn't mean it," I told Renate in school the next day, but she said she wasn't allowed to play with me anymore and walked away.

Her limp seemed worse than ever before, and I felt as if I had caused it. If only I could take back the words. During recess, she stood alone in the schoolyard, eating an apple. My hands in the pockets of my pleated skirt, I leaned against the fence close by, feeling hollow despite the cheese sandwich I'd just eaten. If only she'd call me something real bad, something worse than gimp. Even if she said that my parents had found me at the dump, or that my mother should have thrown me away as a baby because I was too ugly to keep—I pushed my fists deeper into my pockets, jammed back my elbows into the diamond-shaped holes in the fence.

After school I waited for her outside the building. "Do you want to buy some licorice?"

She shook her head.

"I still have my allowance."

"I'm not hungry."

"We could ride bikes."

"I have to go home." She crossed the street.

I followed her on the opposite sidewalk. Mist hung low above the streets and garden walls, yet left the trees and houses untouched. Frau Weskopp passed us on her bicycle, her black coat flapping around her. I could tell she was on her way to the cemetery because a watering can dangled from her handlebar. When Renate reached her front door, she turned around as if she wanted to make sure I was close by before she slipped inside.

I left my books at our house and walked toward the river. The streets were damp; it had rained nearly every day that April. When I got close to the Tegerns' house, the architect's seven German shepherds threw themselves against the chain-link fence, barking. The skin above their gums was drawn back, and their teeth glistened. Though Renate and I always ran past the fence, I made myself stop on the sidewalk, close enough to smell the wet fur and see the strings of saliva on the dogs' tongues. I snarled back at them. The hair on their backs rose as they scrambled across each other, trying to climb up the fence, barking and howling at me.

"Cowards," I hissed, wishing Renate could see me. I raised my hands, curled my fingers into claws. "Cowards."

A curtain shifted in the window above the solarium and Frau Tegern knocked against the glass, motioning me away as if afraid for me or, perhaps, herself. I gave the dogs one final ferocious growl and turned my back to them.

Along the river the mist was thicker, and the water looked brown-green, darker than the meadow where a herd of sheep grazed. I heard the tearing of grass blades as their teeth closed around them. The shapes of poplars and willows were blurred. Above the water line the rocks were gray and damp, the upper ones splotched with a white crust.

Frau Brocker used to bring Rolf and me to the river when we were small. While she smoked one of her Gauloises, Rolf and I searched for scraps of paper and dry leaves, packing them into the crevices between the stones before setting a match to them.

I sat on a boulder and dug my sneakers into the heaps of pebbles around me. Maybe if I gave Renate a present . . . I could let her have my radio. Or any of the dolls in my room. I didn't play with them anyhow. But neither did Renate. I picked up a pebble, tried to flit it across the waves; it sank without rising once. Perhaps we could switch bicycles. She liked mine better than hers. It had even been touched by holy water at the pastor's last blessing of the vehicles and didn't have any rust on it.

If I were Renate, the thing I'd want most in the world—it was so simple—her leg, of course, her left leg, to have it grow and fill out like the other one. I thought of my Oma's healer—not even a saint—who'd touched her leg and dissolved a blood clot in the artery below her knee. Oma had told me it was as much her belief in the healing as the healing itself that had saved her leg from having to be amputated. Miracles happened that way. Even without saints. As long as you believed in them. I bent to search for a flat, round pebble and found a white one with amber veins. After spitting on it for luck, I skipped it across the water. It sprang up in wide arcs four, five . . . a total of eight times.

That evening I looked around our cellar for an empty bottle. Our housekeeper stored things there which she said she might use some day: cardboard boxes with old magazines and brochures, empty bottles and jars, a four-liter pot with a hole in the bottom, a stained lampshade, even the tin tub I'd been bathed in until I was two. Most of the bottles were too large, but finally I found an empty vinegar bottle behind the washing machine.

I soaked off the label, rinsed the inside, and hid it in my room until Wednesday morning when St. Martin's Church was empty because Mass was held at the chapel. The bottle in my knapsack, I sneaked into the side door of the church early before school. In the morning light the blond wood of the pews gleamed as if someone had rubbed it with oil. The stale scent of incense made it hard to breathe. Though I knew Herr Pastor Beier was at the chapel two kilometers away, I kept glancing toward the purple curtains of the confessional.

Marble steps with a red runner led to the altar, which was built of solid black marble. Centered between two silver bowls with tulips stood five candles thicker than Renate's legs. From *The Last Supper* mural above the altar, the dark eyes of Jesus and the apostles traced my movements. I'd heard enough stories about church robbers to know the wrath of God could strike at any moment and leave me dead on the floor. As I walked toward the back of the church to the basin of holy water, the white veins in the marble floor reached for my feet like the nets of a fisherman.

Quickly I submerged my vinegar bottle in the cold water. Silver bubbles rose to the surface as the bottle filled—much too slowly. On the wide balcony above me, I felt the silent weight of the organ pipes.

"You want to come to my house?" I whispered to Renate as I followed her out of school that afternoon.

She shook her head and kept walking, tilting to the left with each step, her white knee socks bunched around her ankles.

"It's about a surprise."

She glanced at me sideways. "What is it?"

"I can't tell." My knapsack over one arm, I continued walking next to her. "I have to show it to you."

"Why?"

"Because. It's a secret."

"What if I don't want it?"

"You will. I swear."

She stopped. "Is it a harmonica?"

"Better."

"Better than a kitten?"

"Much better."

"Better than—"

"The best thing that could happen to you," I promised.

She still had some doubt in her eyes as we took the steps down to our cellar. I thought of the nights my mother and grandmother had hidden there with neighbors while the wail of sirens pierced the dark. The war had ended a year before Renate and I were born. Several kids in our school had lost their fathers at the Russian front. Adults never mentioned the war unless we asked about it, and then they fled into vague sentences about a dark period for Germany. "Nobody wants to relive those years," they'd say gravely. My mother was the only one who answered some of our questions and told us about the terror of air raids, the hunger and cold everyone had suffered.

"Sit over there." I pointed to the crates next to the apple shelves. Every fall my father and I filled those crates with apples we'd picked at an orchard in Krefeld. Afterward we'd wrap the apples in newspaper and lay them on the shelves. It was my job to rotate them every two weeks, sorting out the rotten ones, so the others would last through the winter.

Renate sat on the crate closest to the door. The wall at the far end of the cellar was still black, right up to the two high windows that were blind with layers of coal dust and cobwebs. Until the oil furnace had been installed two years before, I used to help my father stack coal briquettes to within a hand's width of the window.

I picked up the other crate and moved it in front of Renate. "You have to take off your left shoe and sock."

"Why?" She straightened her shoulders.

"Because. It's part of it. You'll see." I took the bottle from my knapsack.

Renate pulled her bare foot from the cement floor. "It's cold."

I sat down on the crate across from her. "Let me have your leg." When she hesitated, I whispered, "I've figured out a way to make it all right—your leg, I mean—heal it."

She swallowed hard. "How?"

"It'll be like your other leg."

She drew her lower lip between her teeth, but then she raised her left leg and, carefully, laid her bare foot on my knees. It was a pale foot, a thin foot with toenails longer than mine, a foot that felt warm and sweaty as I put one hand around it to keep her from yanking it back.

With my teeth I uncorked the bottle. "All you need to do is close your eyes and believe it will work."

"What's in there?" Renate stared at me.

"Holy water." I poured some of it into my palm. It felt cold and smelled musty.

"Wait." She reached into her mouth with her right forefinger and thumb and took out a pink wad of chewing gum. After sticking it on the side of her crate, she closed her eyes and raised her face as though about to receive Communion.

I rubbed the holy water up and down Renate's calf, between her toes, along the arch of her foot. Light filtered in uneven splotches from the dust-smeared light bulb above us. I've always had an enormous capacity to believe. Stories, miracles, lies—with the right details, I can be convinced of the authenticity of nearly anything, even *Hasenbrot*, rabbit bread, which my father brought me many evenings when he returned from working on people's teeth. Handing me half a sandwich wrapped in oil-stained brown paper, he'd tell me that on his way home he'd seen a *Hase*, a rabbit, by the side of the road, carrying this package—he'd motion to the sandwich—between its front paws. He leapt from his car to catch it, but the *Hase* ran off with the bundle; my father followed it across the brook and chased it along Schreberstrasse until the *Hase* finally dropped the package next to the brook and disappeared. The bundle was about to slide into the water when my father saw it.

Every time my father chased the *Hase* through a different area, and every time there was that one breath-catching moment when the bundle was almost lost all over again because a car nearly ran over it or a dog tried to tear it from his hands. I'd unfold the brown paper with something bordering on reverence. Though the bread was always a bit stale, the meat limp, and the cheese soggy, I've never tasted anything as delicious as my father's *Hasenbrot*.

And it was with that kind of faith that I dribbled holy water over Renate's foot and leg. I kneaded it into the crescent-shaped callus at her heel, into the bony disk of her knee. Her teeth had released her lower lip, and she breathed evenly.

Already I felt a difference in her leg: the skin seemed warmer and didn't look as pale anymore. With each day her leg would stretch itself, grow fuller, stronger. It would be able to keep up with the other leg when she pedaled her bike. She'd play hopscotch. Tag.

"You can look now."

Renate blinked, staring at me, then at her leg.

"See?" I bent over her leg, my heart fast.

Cautiously she probed her ankle with her fingertips, then her calf. "I think so."

"It's already begun to change."

"Are you sure?"

"Absolutely."

"Should we do it again tomorrow? To make double sure?"

"No," I said, instinctively knowing the difference between a miracle and a treatment. "All you need to do is believe it worked."

She raised her leg from my knees. "It feels different."

"See?"

"What do we do with the rest of the holy water?"

I hadn't even thought of that. The bottle was still half full. It didn't feel right to pour it out or leave it here in the basement.

"We could drink it," Renate suggested.

I felt as if the eyes of the apostles were watching me as I raised the bottle to my lips, swallowed, and gave it to Renate who drank and handed it back to me. It tasted the way damp stones smell and within an hour I had stomach cramps, punishment, no doubt, for stealing holy water, a sin I didn't dare confess.

Over the next weeks I watched for signs of change in Renate's left leg. I pictured the pores closing, the skin losing its chalky color, the calf filling out.

"Does it feel different?" I'd ask her, and she'd nod and say, "I think so."

The end of April we took our bicycles to the annual blessing of vehicles on the Burgdorf fairgrounds where Herr Pastor Beier sprinkled holy water on cars, trucks, tractors, motor scooters, and bikes to keep them in good condition and out of accidents. Renate still couldn't keep up with me as we rode back to her house. By then the midwife had accepted my apology and welcomed me back into her house, all the time cleaning up behind us.

In July Renate and I picked purple clover blossoms on the fairgrounds and watched the gypsies set up their tents and booths. I found myself staring at their faces, afraid to discover resemblances between Renate and them, relieved when I didn't. We rode the merry-go-round, ate white sausages with mustard, threw Ping-Pong balls through wooden loops. The biggest tent had been set up for the circus, and Renate's mother took Adi and us to the Saturday performance. We applauded when five fat clowns tumbled out of a tiny car, when the animal tamer stuck his head inside the lion's mouth, and when the elephants circled the arena, their trunks holding the tails of the elephants ahead of them.

During intermission Adi bought us candied apples, and when we returned to our seats, the lights dimmed. It turned dark inside the tent, and the voices faded into whispers, then silence. High above us a slow shimmer began to spread. It came from a woman with black hair who stood on the tightrope in a short golden dress. I felt Renate's hand on my arm; her fingers were dry, warm. The woman's arms and legs shimmered as she set one foot in front of the other and crossed the wide gap.

If there were nets that day in the circus, Renate and I didn't see them. We believed the woman was safe. It had to do with faith. We had proven that to ourselves that afternoon in the cellar when the holy water had worked after all, not healing Renate's leg but the rift between us. Some acts of faith, I believe, have the power to grant us something infinitely wiser than what we imagine. We all have our props for faith, and the shakier the faith, the more props we need. But sometimes the faith is strong enough so that an old vinegar bottle with holy water and a crate next to the apple shelves will do.

EL DIABLO DE LA CIENEGA

Geoffrey Becker

The black sports car that pulled up in a puff of dust alongside the La Cienega Community Center looked like a big hand, placed palm down in the red dirt. Ignoring it, Victor kept his feet in front of the chalked line on the cracked concrete. The door clicked open and a very tanned man with straw-colored hair got out, stuck his hands into the pockets of his chinos, and leaned back to watch. No time left on the clock, Spurs down by one. As always, the game had come down to this one deciding moment. Victor made the first shot, then lobbed up the second for the win. There had never really been any doubt. Just for the hell of it, he made them again.

The late afternoon sun glinted off the broken windshields of a half-dozen wrecked and rusting cars across the road. Beyond them sat nine mobile homes, all in poor repair, set at odd angles to each other. The community center, a square building with flaking yellow stucco and one intact window, sported a tiny sign indicating that it had also once served as the

45

La Cienega Volunteer Fire Department. From the south wall, a faded outline of a mural of the Virgin someone had begun long ago and never finished gazed out, faceless. The building was abandoned but, with the exception of a few weedy cracks in its surface, the basketball court alongside it was still in good shape.

Victor looked over briefly at the man, then continued shooting. He tossed in seven consecutive baskets before one finally circled the rim and hopped back out.

"Hope I didn't make you nervous," called the man.

Victor, twelve, had recently experienced a growth spurt that had turned him into a gangly, stretched-out cartoon of what he'd looked like the year before. He was particularly sensitive to criticism. Catching the ball, he responded by spinning around and executing a perfect hook shot that touched nothing but net. He turned and faced the man.

"Victor Garcia?"

"Sure," said Victor.

"I've heard about you." The man got up from where he was leaning and walked onto the court. He wore a pink Lacoste shirt and Top-Siders. The license plate on his car said Texas. "I like to shoot a little hoop myself now and then. Usually, when I go someplace new, I ask around to find out who's good."

Victor eyed him with suspicion, but also a certain amount of pride. It was, after all, about time he got some attention.

"Fact."

"Who'd you ask?"

He waved his hand in the general direction from which he'd come. "Guy up the road."

"Lopez?"

"I think he said his name was Lopez. What's the difference? He was right. You've got the touch. Not everybody does, you know. Just the right balance of things—you concentrate well, but you're relaxed, too."

Victor glanced across the street, where a tiny dust devil spun in the yard in front of Rodriguez's place. "What are you, CIA?" he asked.

The man shook his head and chuckled. "Close, though. FOA. Ferrari Owners of America."

"Ferrari? That's what this is?"

The man smiled, his lips drawing back to reveal a set of china-white teeth, and waved toward his car. "You have to pass a stupidity test to qualify for one. Getting parts is murder. On my fourth clutch. I'm up here for a convention. Southwest chapter—we're meeting in Santa Fe this year. I always try to drive around and see the country a little. It's beautiful out here—all these extinct volcanoes. Kind of violent, if you know what I mean. You're lucky to live where you do."

"I guess," Victor said, dubiously. He didn't feel particularly lucky.

"I mean it. Look around. It's true what they say about northern New Mexico. There's a quality to the light. Sky's as blue as a polished gemstone. What do you all say? 'The Land of Enchantment?'" He raised his hands as if demonstrating a magic trick, then smiled and indicated that Victor should give him the ball, which he did. He bounced it once, then took a shot—a perfect swish. The hairs on his muscled arms stood high off the skin, making him appear to have a kind of golden aura. Victor retrieved the ball.

"Nice," he said, passing it back. Phony as blue macaroni, he thought to himself, which was something Rodriguez liked to say. A hunk of old metal tubing lay on the ground a few feet away, and Victor figured if he needed, he could probably get to it quick enough to inflict some damage.

47

The stranger eyed the basket and did it again.

"Victor Garcia," he said, walking over to get the ball from the pile of rubble where it had rolled. "Are you a betting man?"

"I got nothing to bet," Victor said.

"That's OK. We can negotiate. I just think it might be fun to have a little competition—you and me. Friendly."

He decided the stranger was harmless. "Free throws?"

"Maybe. Maybe something a little more challenging."

A car came up the road, its muffler dragging noisily on the dirt and gravel. Victor's mother was returning home from the motel where she changed sheets.

"I got to go," Victor said, taking back his ball, though reluctantly. He would have liked to show this man what he could do.

From his pocket, the man withdrew a black leather wallet, and out of that he took a business card which he handed to Victor. It read: E. Crispin Light, Import/Export.

"Most of my friends just call me Money," he said. "It's my basketball name."

"Money?"

"You know—money in the bank. Kind of like Bill Bradley was 'Dollar Bill.'"

Victor looked again at the card. The printing on it was in gold. "What does the *E* stand for?"

"Good, good," said Money, grinning. "Most people don't even ask. The fact is, it doesn't stand for anything. I put it on there because I think it looks classy. What do you think?"

Victor shrugged. Across the road, he could see his mom struggling with groceries. "You coming back?"

"You bet." Money looked at his watch. "Tomorrow evening. Will you be here?"

"I'm always here," said Victor, coolly.

"All right. You go on home now and look after your mom."

Victor shielded his eyes against a sudden gust of wind that threw a curtain of dust up around them. "What do you know about my mom?"

"Did I say I knew anything?" He smiled. "I'll see you tomorrow, Victor." He shook the boy's hand. His was hard and calloused as if, even though he appeared to be rich, he still did a fair amount of manual labor. Gardening, maybe, Victor thought. The man got back into his car and drove off in the direction of the setting sun.

The understanding came to him clearly, in the middle of the night, when he awoke to the sound of his mother's coughing. This was a nightly occurrence—the luminous readout on his alarm clock said 3:06, and as he lay waiting for the sounds to subside, he was filled with a mixture of fear and pride. He really was good. Not just good the way anyone who practices enough can become good, but special.

He got up and went into the kitchen to make himself a cocktail, his name for the milk, Nestle's Quik, and raw egg drink he'd invented as part of his personal training regimen. From her bedroom, his mother continued to cough, a deep, body-racking sound that seemed to originate in her stomach and work its way up.

Taking his drink, he unlocked the door and stepped outside. There were stars everywhere, more than he'd ever seen. In the darkness, the shapes of the wrecked cars were ominous, lurking monsters. Victor walked toward them, if only to prove to himself he wasn't scared. Something moved on one of the hoods and he halted. Gradually, his eyes became more accustomed to the light and he saw a small lizard. It was watching him.

"It's you, isn't it?" he said.

The lizard did not move. Even out here, the sound of his mother's hacking was clearly audible, the only disturbance in the night's solemn quiet.

"I'm ready to deal," said Victor. "I know who you are. I know what you want. I'm not afraid. If I lose, you can have my soul, to be damned to eternal hellfire. But if I win, I want you to make my mom OK again." He paused for a moment, considering whether to throw in something else, too, like a million dollars, or a starting position with the San Antonio Spurs, but it seemed to him that if he were fighting the forces of darkness, it would be best to keep his own motives as pure and true as possible. "Tomorrow," he said. "Sundown."

The lizard continued to look at him. Then, to Victor's astonishment, it nodded its head once and scurried away.

As he passed his mother's door on his way back to bed, Victor stopped and whispered, "It's all right. I'm taking care of everything."

But E. Crispin Light did not appear the next evening. Victor spent over two hours on the basketball court, dribbling, shooting, working on the basics, keeping his eye out for the black sports car. It was too bad, because his shooting was dead accurate—he hit nineteen out of twenty from the free-throw line. He felt certain he could have beaten all comers, even an emissary from the Prince of Darkness. Eventually, as the light began to fade, he put his ball under one arm and walked home.

His mother was watching *Wheel of Fortune*.

"If only I could spell a little better," she lamented. "I'd go to Hollywood and clean up on this game." She held a small clay pot in one hand, a paintbrush in the other. She picked up extra money painting Anasazi designs onto local pottery for sale to tourists. She was very pale. Victor's father had been Mexican, but his mother was from California, a thin woman of Irish extraction, with large, sad eyes. Though she'd been sick now on and off for the better part of a year, she refused to go to a doctor. They had no insurance. Her one gesture toward her health had been to quit smoking, but it had only seemed to make the coughing worse. She held out a pot. "Want to try one?"

Victor shook his head. "I'm thinking," he said.

"What you need is some friends," she said. "You spend too much time alone."

"I don't need no friends," he said.

"Any. 'I don't need any friends.'" She raised her eyebrows, then drew a line around the lip of the vase. "Alabaster caught a lizard this morning. Tore the poor thing to bits."

Victor swallowed hard. "A lizard?"

"You know. One of those grayish ones."

Alabaster, who was part Persian, lay in the windowsill, cleaning her paws. Victor stared at her, trying to see if she looked any different. After all, he reasoned, it might have been any lizard.

"Are you all right?" asked his mother. "You look a little pale."

"I'm fine," he said. "How are you?"

"Oh, on a scale of one to ten, today was about a four, I'd say."

"It's going to get better," he told her. Then he excused himself and went to his room.

The plaza in Santa Fe was filled with Ferraris, all of them polished to a radiance, reflecting sunlight, smelling richly of gasoline and leather. They were arranged by year and model—

scores of them parked side to side, their owners hovering about, keeping a wary eye out for people who might ignore the "Do Not Touch" signs in their windshields. Victor locked his bicycle and wandered among the automobiles, looking for one in particular. After making almost a complete circuit of the plaza, he found it, wedged in among six others of exactly the same style, but the only black one with Texas plates. He looked around for Money, but he was not in the immediate area. Victor peered in, cupping his hands to the tinted glass, half-expecting to see a dance of writhing, tortured souls. The inside did look like another world, but only a wealthy one. The control panel was polished walnut, the seats a deep, red leather. There was a Willie Nelson cassette in the tape deck, a New Mexico highway map on the dashboard. A little disappointed, he stuck his hands in his pockets and turned.

"Hello, Victor." For a Texan, Money had almost no accent at all. He wore sunglasses and a maroon golf shirt.

"What happened?" said Victor. "You didn't come."

"Yeah, sorry about that. We had a big dinner at the hotel and it got late. I'll make it up to you."

Victor tried to seem as though he didn't care. "You're the one wanted to come and shoot."

"I realize that, and I feel badly about it. If I'd had your number, I would have called."

Victor didn't mention that for the past two months, as a part of an economizing measure, they'd been doing without a phone. He thought again of the lizard. "You were where?"

"At a dinner. That's what we do at these conventions. We drive our cars to some central location, then hang around eating and drinking. It's pretty boring, really, but it gets me out of the office. Buy you an ice cream?"

Victor accepted, and the two of them took their cones to a bench.

Money took off his glasses. "Have you decided what you want to play for?"

Victor met his eyes, which seemed to him like cold, blue stones. He thought of the devil movies he'd seen. It seemed a peculiar question. "Do I have a choice?"

"There's always a choice. Only remember, never get into a bet you're not prepared to lose."

"I'm not going to lose. And you're going to help my mother."

"What are you suggesting, Victor?"

"She can't sleep, and she's got trouble with her breathing."

"Then she ought to see a doctor."

"Give her back her health," said Victor. "If I win, that's what I want."

He took out a set of black driving gloves and swatted a fly that had landed on his knee. "And if I win?"

"You can have my soul."

Money arched an eyebrow. "Your soul?"

Victor nodded. "You heard me."

"Big stakes."

"Yes."

Money thought this over for a moment. He bit into the cone part of his ice cream and chewed noisily, then swallowed. "I think you may have mistaken me for someone else. I'm only a businessman who likes to play a little ball. But all right, you're on."

Just then, a man with a bullhorn made an announcement.

"That's my category," said Money. "Let's go see if I won anything."

Victor followed him to where a man in a plaid jacket stood next to a blonde lady in a white jumpsuit, carrying a clipboard.

She took the bullhorn and announced the winner's name, and a fat man in a brown cowboy hat jumped up to accept the plaque.

Victor watched Money's reaction, expecting to see anger, possibly rage. The potential seemed there—behind Money's cool, sculpted face, there was a hint of something smoldering, competitive and mean. But he just shook his head.

"These things are all fixed," he said. "I don't even know why I bother."

The evening was a hot one, with only the vaguest hint of a breeze from the southwest. Victor was out on the court early, dribbling around, working on his bank shot. True to his word, Money appeared a little after seven, his black car still shiny as glass in spite of the dust its tires kicked up. The engine roared and was silent.

He was dressed in worn blue gym shorts and a red tank top, and his sneakers were red canvas high-tops from another era. He was muscled and trim, but he looked very human, and for a minute, Victor wondered if he might be wrong about him. Maybe he really was what he claimed, just a rich guy who liked to play basketball. But the devil could be a trickster—he knew that from Rodriguez's woman, Opal, whose entire life seemed to be made up of encounters with him. The Evil One took a special interest, she said, in tormenting her. Just last week, a mysterious wind had taken a sheet off her clothesline and hung it from the branches of a nearby cottonwood, where it flapped like a sail for two days because Opal refused to have anything to do with it. She'd finally given Victor fifty cents to climb up and get it.

Money tossed a basketball to Victor, who caught it and examined its material and make. Leather, with no visible trademark—good grain, easy to grip. He bounced it and took a set shot which fell two feet short of the basket. He adjusted and proceeded to put the next five into the net. "I'm ready," he said.

"We'll play Death," said Money. "A game of accuracy. Shoot to go first."

"Don't you want to warm up?"

"I'm always warm. Go ahead."

Victor took a foul shot and sank it. Then Money went to the line, crouched with the ball under his chin, eyed the basket and shot. The ball bounced off the rim.

Victor grinned. "Maybe you should have warmed up."

"Your shot," said Money.

Victor figured he'd go for it, right from the start. He walked off the court, over to where the Ferrari was parked, and from there put up a long, high, arching shot. It looped three times around the rim and flew out.

"Don't be too cocky," said Money. "Rule number one." He collected the ball, dribbled out to a crack in the pavement where the top of the key would have been and executed a turn-around jumper that fell perfectly through the hole.

Victor took the ball and repeated the shot. Still, he was furious with himself for giving up the advantage. Now, he was on the defensive, forced to wait for his opponent to miss.

Shot for shot, they were both perfect. Money did a backward lay-up, but Victor easily made one too. Fall-away jumpers, hook shots, they each sank everything they put up. Finally, after nearly five minutes, a sloppy jump shot gave the advantage back to Victor. He put in a twenty-foot banker. Money whistled, walked to the spot, and did the same. Rather than try something else, Victor took the shot again—he had a sense that he'd make it, and he figured he'd keep going from the same place until Money missed. He didn't have to wait. Money's attempt went off the backboard, missing the rim entirely.

"You've got *D*," said Victor, a little louder than he'd intended.

"Just shoot the ball," said Money.

It went on, a slow game, a game of nerves and of strategy. Money kept trying to distract him.

"Are you worried? I know I would be. You've got a lot at stake here."

"I'm not scared," said Victor. In fact, he was getting a little nervous. He'd never thought the contest would last this long.

"But your soul. That's a big wager. Maybe you're betting over your head."

"You don't scare me."

"I'm not trying to scare you. I'm trying to let you know that I appreciate the seriousness of your convictions. For me, basketball has always just been a game. I don't let it obsess me the way you do. That's why I'm going to win, because I have less at stake. I'm more relaxed."

"If it was just a game to you, how come you came out here to find me?" Victor went to the foul line, stood with his back to the basket, and put the ball in backward, over his head.

"Well," said Money, "isn't that special?" He tried the shot and missed.

"*D-E* for you," said Victor.

Within a few minutes, Victor started missing shots, ones he should have been making. Money played with an icy calm, calculating his shots like geometry problems. It was as if, Victor thought, unseen forces were acting upon him, making him miss. To make matters worse, each time he did, Money smiled at him and said "thunk." Pretty soon, Victor was behind, with three letters. Glancing over at the Ferrari, he saw that Alabaster was curled up on the hood, sunning herself. It was, he thought, a very bad sign.

"We can quit now," said Money. "I don't mind."

"No way."

"Don't kid yourself, Victor. You're going to lose, in spite of that name of yours. But it doesn't matter. There's nothing magical about being a good basketball player. It won't do anything for you down the road, other than make you wish you spent your time on something more useful. You'll never be a great—you've got no killer instinct. And you're too short."

"Stop talking," said Victor.

"Just trying to get you to be realistic."

Just then, one of Rodriguez's dogs got loose, ran across the street, and began barking at the stranger. Money froze in the middle of the court as the black-and-white mongrel bared her teeth and snarled, tail flat down as if she expected at any moment to be kicked. Rodriguez himself appeared after about a minute, a beer in his hand, to grab the dog by the collar.

"Who's winning?" he asked.

"That's one fierce hound," said Money, nervously keeping his distance. "Hunter?"

"No hunter," said Rodriguez. "She's a lover. Just had her third litter this year." He pursed his lips, eyeing this stranger with the nice car. "You want some puppies?"

"No, thanks," said Money.

"Ten bucks," said Rodriguez. He was a squat, muscular man, with a hank of hair that dangled loosely over his forehead.

"I don't much like dogs."

"No, man. Ten bucks the kid beats you."

"Well. Ten bucks it is," said Money. "Where were we?"

"My shot," said Victor. Think no bad thoughts, he told himself. Keep your heart pure. He put in a running hook.

Money made his hook, picked up his own rebound, and bounced the ball back to Victor.

"I need another beer," announced Rodriguez, and dragged the dog back across the street. He returned moments later with a six-pack and settled in the dirt by the side of the court to watch. After a little while, he was joined by Opal, her heavyset, Navajo features almost making it seem as if she were wearing a mask. She broke open one of the beers and tipped her head back to receive the contents.

Over by the trailers, the competition across the road was attracting attention. Many of the residents began to emerge to see what was going on. The two long-hair drunks whom everyone called Manny and Moe, and who worked as part-time construction workers when they weren't sleeping off the booze, walked slow circles around Money's car, nodding their heads and making approving comments. Distracted by them, or maybe just growing tired, Money bounced one off the rim.

"That's *D-E-A*," said Rodriguez, who had appointed himself referee.

"I know what it is," said Money. "Please, don't touch the car."

There was now a small crowd gathered—nearly fifteen people. Somebody brought out potato chips and passed them around. Victor felt as if he were in a spotlight. These were people who generally ignored each other, except for a nod in passing, but there was a real sense of community as they watched the contest. Last to come out was Victor's mother. Shielding her eyes against the slanted light, she looked pale and ghostlike. The wind, which was beginning to pick up as it always did at this time of day, tossed her housedress around her knees.

Victor did a reverse lay-up. There was a smattering of applause.

The sweat stood out on Money's face as he bounced the ball in preparation. Then he moved under the basket and flipped the ball backward over his head. As he did so, one ankle buckled and he went tumbling forward onto the pavement.

"Damn," he said, holding the ankle in front of him like a foreign object. He kneaded it for a few moments, then hobbled to his feet.

"*D-E-A-T*," sang Rodriguez. "Uh-oh."

Victor considered. Repeating the lay-up would finish Money off easily—with his twisted ankle, he wouldn't have a chance. But it seemed like a cheap ending, and Victor had an audience. He wanted to do something spectacular.

"Everything on this shot," he heard himself say.

"Everything?" Money said, cautiously. "Are you sure?"

"Everything."

"Done," said Money.

"What are you guys playing for, anyway?" asked Rodriguez. When there was no answer, he shrugged and opened another beer.

Victor walked the ball right off the court, out into the dirt lot beyond it, a few feet from a particularly nasty-looking cholla. The crowd let out a cheerful noise, encouraging, but with laughter mixed in—no one believed for a moment that the wiry, sad-faced twelve year old could possibly hurl a ball that far, let alone make it go through a hoop. Money hobbled around in obvious pain, but the look of amusement on his face was unmistakable.

Victor knew the moment he looked at the basket and saw how far he was away, that this was impossible. He'd overdone it—he was way beyond his range. But he couldn't see any way out now without losing face. In his hands the ball seemed to gain weight, as if it were filling internally with liquid. Money was still smiling at him. His neighbors watched in anticipation. His mother stood among them, her hands clenched in fists at her sides. He'd blown it, he told himself. He'd failed to stay pure. Pride was one of the seven deadly sins (he was pretty sure about this), and his own had brought him to the brink of the abyss.

Holding the ball to his chest, he gauged the distance to the net and prayed for a miracle. He did not want to die. He tried to imagine what it would be like to spend eternity soulless, in a box, no air, no light, the rough wood pressed up against his face. For a moment, he felt as if his feet had grown roots and that his bones extended deep down into the earth, into places damp, fungal, and cool. Then he put the ball as high into the air as he could possibly throw it.

Moving in what seemed like slow motion, the ball described an orange-brown arc, at the very top of which it hung for a moment, certain to fall short. Then, out of the south, a powerful wind kicked up, and for a moment, the whole world seemed to shake. Tumbleweed rolled around the court, and the rim of Rodriguez's beer can was coated with red-brown dust. Descending on the shoulders of the wind, the ball actually cleared the basket, arriving first at the backboard, then glancing smoothly down through the net.

Victor screamed at the top of his lungs, and his voice was joined by a chorus of others from across the road.

"Never happen again in a million years," said Rodriguez, walking onto the court.

"Lucky," said Money, shaking his head.

"Hey, man," said Rodriguez. "He beat you square and fair. Pay up."

Money hobbled over to his car and brought back a wallet. He took out a ten and gave it to Rodriguez.

"You don't owe the kid no cash?" asked Rodriguez.

"No," said Money. "I don't."

"So, what then?"

Money shrugged and shook Victor's hand, then went back to his car and got in.

"What about our deal?" said Victor. He felt suddenly anxious, more so than he had during the game.

Money leaned his head out the window and looked at him long and hard. "I never expected to lose," he said at last. His tinted window hummed and closed, leaving Victor staring at his own reflection. Then the Ferrari's engine fired, coughing dust out around the back tires. Spewing gravel behind him, Money pulled out onto the street and headed in the direction of the county road.

"Texans," said Rodriguez. "Think they own the world." He spat into the dirt. "You shoot pretty good basketball, my friend. But you don't know the first thing about gambling." He turned and headed back, Opal following at his heels. Across the street, most of the onlookers had already returned to their trailers.

Victor's mother put a hand on his head. "Did you bet with that man?" she asked.

Victor said nothing.

"What did you bet?"

He didn't answer. The wind that had come and carried his shot home was gone, and in its place, the evening crept in, cool and still.

She shook her head in frustration. "I don't know what it is with you these days," she said. "I don't know what you're thinking." She put her forehead up against his and stared directly into his eyes, but he was silent. "Don't stay out too long," she told him finally. She walked back across the street.

Alone now on the court, Victor saw that Money had left his ball. It sat in the dirt, near where his car had been parked. He picked it up and bounced it a few times, the smack it made against the concrete seeming to echo off the surrounding hills, a lonely, casual sound. He felt cheated. Still, something had happened—he knew that. He would not allow himself the easy luxury of disappointment. For a brief moment, the powers of the universe had convened in his fingertips. He watched the lights come on in the different trailers, listened to the sounds of Opal and Rodriguez starting up one of their nightly arguments. He bounced the ball a few more times in the dimming light, watching his shadow move against the pavement, taller than any man's and growing longer with each passing minute.

THE CAT AND THE COFFEE DRINKERS

Max Steele

Only the five-year-old children who were sent to the kindergarten of Miss Effie Barr had any idea what they were learning in that one-room schoolhouse, and they seldom told anyone, and certainly not grown people.

My father was sent to her when he was five years old, and thirty years later when no one had much money, I was sent to her. Even though ours was no longer a small Southern town, and even though she was already in her seventies the first time I saw her, Miss Effie had known all the children in her school a year, and often longer, before they appeared before her for lessons. My mother, with proper gloves and hat, began taking me to call on her when I was four.

It was a good place to visit. The house was a large gray one with elegant white columns, and it was set well back from the same street we lived on. Until the Depression the Barrs had owned the entire block and theirs was the only house on it.

There were mossy brick steps leading up from the hitching post to the gravel walk which curved between overgrown boxwoods to the low porch with its twelve slender columns. There in the summer in the shade of the water oaks Miss Effie, dressed in black, would be sitting, knitting or embroidering while her big gray cat sat at, and sometimes on, her feet. Slow uncertain music would be coming through the open windows from the music room, where her older sister, Miss Hattie, gave piano lessons.

Miss Effie never seemed to watch a child on such visits, or offer him anything like cookies or lemonade, or say anything to endear herself to a youngster. Instead she would talk lady-talk with the mother and, hardly pausing, say to the waiting child, "You can pull up the wild onions on the lawn if you've nothing better to do." There was no suggestion in her voice that it was a game or that there would be a reward. She simply stated what could be done if one took a notion. Usually a child did.

There was no nonsense about Miss Effie. One morning in late September my mother and I were standing with eleven other mothers and children on the wide porch. Miss Effie looked everyone over carefully from where she stood with one hand on the screen door. She checked a list in the other hand against the faces on the porch to be sure that these were the children she had chosen from the forty or more who had visited her in the summer.

Apparently satisfied, or at least reconciled to another year of supplementing her income (for no Southern lady of her generation "worked"), she opened the door wide and said in her indifferent tone, "Children inside." When one mother tried to lead her reluctant son into the dark parlor, Miss Effie said, "Mothers outside." She pushed the big cat out with her foot and said, "You too, Mr. Thomas."

When the children were all inside and the mothers outside, Miss Effie latched the screen, thanked the mothers for bringing the children, and reminded them that classes began at eight thirty and ended at noon. The tuition of two dollars a week would be acceptable each Friday, and each child as part of his training should be given the responsibility for delivering the money in an envelope bearing the parent's signature. She thanked them again in such a way that there was nothing for them to do except wander together in a group down the gravel walk.

Miss Effie then turned to us, standing somewhat closer together than was necessary in the center of the dark parlor, and said, "Since this is your first day, I want to show you everything. Then you won't be wondering about things while you should be listening."

She made us look at the Oriental carpet, the grandfather clock, the bookcases of leather-bound volumes, and the shelves on which were collections of rocks, shells, birds' nests, and petrified wood. She offered to let us touch, just this once, any of these things.

She would not let us into the music room, but she indicated through the door the imported grand piano, the red plush seat where Miss Hattie sat during lessons, the music racks, the ferns, and the window seats, which she said were full of sheet music. "You're never to go in there," she said. "I don't go in there myself."

Next, she showed us the dining room, the den, and the hallway, and then at the foot of the stairs she said, "We're going upstairs, and then you'll never go up there again." Barbara Ware, one of the three girls, began to whimper. "Don't worry," Miss Effie said. "You'll come back down. But there'll be no reason to go up again. I want you to see everything so you won't have to ask personal questions, which would certainly be the height of impoliteness, wouldn't it? I mean, if you started wanting to know, without my telling you, where I sleep and which window is Miss Hattie's, I'd think you were rude, wouldn't I? I'll show you everything so you won't be tempted to ask personal questions."

We went up the stairs, and she showed us her room and where she kept her shoes (in the steps leading up to the side of the four-poster bed), where she hung her clothes (in two large wardrobes), and where she kept her hatbox (in a teakwood sea chest). The cat, she said, slept on the sea chest if he happened to be home at night.

She then knocked on the door of Miss Hattie's room and asked her sister if we might look in. Miss Hattie agreed to a short visit. After that Miss Effie showed us the upstairs bathroom and that the bathtub faucet dripped all night and that was why the towel was kept under it.

Downstairs again, she let us see the new kitchen, which was built in 1900, and the back porch, which had been screened in only four years before, with a small door through which the cat could come and go as he liked. We were as fascinated by everything as we would have been if we had never seen a house before.

"Now, out the back door. All of you." She made us all stand on the ground, off the steps, while she lowered herself step by step with the aid of a cane which she kept on a nail by the door. "Now you've seen my house, and you won't see it again. Unless I give your mothers fruitcake and coffee at Christmas. And I don't think I will. Not this year. Do you ever get tired of fruitcake and coffee at Christmas?"

We said we did since it was clear that she did.

"Over there is the barn, and we'll see it some other time. And that is the greenhouse, and we'll be seeing it often. And here is the classroom where we'll be." She pointed with her cane to a square brick building, which before the Civil War had been the kitchen. The door was open.

She shepherded us along the brick walk with her cane, not allowing any of us near enough to her to topple her over. At the open door she said, "Go on in."

We crowded in, and when we were all through the door, she summoned us back out. "Now which of you are boys?" The nine boys raised their hands, following her lead. "And which girls?" The three girls had already separated themselves from the boys and nodded together. "All right then, young gentlemen," she said, regarding us, "let's let the young ladies enter first, or I may think you're all young ladies."

The girls, looking timid and pleased, entered. We started in after them.

"Wait just a minute, young gentlemen," she said. "Haven't you forgotten something?" We looked about for another girl.

"Me!" she announced. "You've forgotten me!" She passed through our huddle, separating us with her stick, and marched into the brick kitchen.

Inside and out, the kitchen was mainly of brick. The walls and floor were brick, and the huge chimney and hearth, except for a closet-cupboard on each side of it, were brick. The ceiling, however, was of beams and broad boards, and the windows were of wavy glass in casements that opened out like shutters. There were three large wooden tables and at each table four chairs.

Again she had to show us everything. The fireplace would be used only in the coldest weather, she said. At other times an

69

iron stove at one side of the room would be used. A captain's chair between the fireplace and the stove was her own and not to be touched by us. A sewing table, overflowing with yarn and knitting needles, was for her own use and not for ours. One cupboard, the one near her, held dishes. She opened its door. She would let us see in the other cupboard later. The tables and chairs and, at the far end of the room, the pegs for coats were all ours to do with as we pleased. It was, she explained, our schoolroom, and therefore, since we were young ladies and gentlemen, she was sure we would keep it clean.

As a matter of fact, she saw no reason why we should not begin with the first lesson: Sweeping and Dusting. She opened the other cupboard and showed us a mop, bucket, rags, brushes, and three brooms. We were not divided into teams; we were not given certain areas to see who could sweep his area cleanest. We were simply told that young ladies should naturally be able to sweep and that young gentlemen at some times in their lives would certainly be expected to sweep a room clean.

The instruction was simple: "You get a good grip on the handle and set to." She handed out the three brooms and started the first three boys sweeping from the fireplace toward the front door. She made simple corrections: "You'll raise a dust, flirting the broom upward. Keep it near the floor. Hold lower on the handle. You'll get more dirt. Don't bend over. You'll be tired before the floor is clean."

Miss Effie corrected the series of sweepers from time to time while she made a big red enamel coffeepot of coffee on a small alcohol stove. Each child was given a turn with the broom before the job was finished. Since the room had not been swept, she admitted, all summer, there was a respectable pile of brick dust, sand, and sweepings near the door by the time she said, "We'll have lunch now." It was already ten o'clock. "After lunch I'll teach you how to take up trash and to dust. Everyone needs to know that."

"Lunch," it happened, was half a mug of coffee each. One spoon of sugar, she said, was sufficient, if we felt it necessary to use sugar at all (she didn't), and there was milk for those who could not or would not (she spoke as though using milk were a defect of character) take their coffee black. I daresay not any of us had ever had coffee before, and Robert Barnes said he hadn't.

"Good!" Miss Effie said. "So you have learned something today."

Miriam Wells, however, said that her parents wouldn't approve of her drinking coffee.

"Very well," Miss Effie said. "Don't drink it. And the next time I offer you any, if I ever do, simply say 'No, thank you, ma'am.'" (The next day Miriam Wells was drinking it along with the rest of us.) "Let's get this clear right this minute—your parents don't need to know what you do when you're under my instruction."

Her firm words gave us a warm feeling, and from that moment on, the schoolroom became a special, safe, and rather secret place.

That day we learned, further, how to rinse out mugs and place them in a pan to be boiled later, how to take up trash, and how to dust. At noon we were taught how to put on our sweaters or coats and how to hold our caps in our left hands until we were outside. We also learned how to approach, one at a time, our teacher (or any lady we should happen to be visiting) and say thank you (for the coffee or whatever we had been served) and how to say goodbye and turn and leave the room without running or laughing.

The next morning Robert Barnes was waiting on his steps when I walked by his house. Since he and I lived nearer to the Barrs than any of the other children, we were the first to arrive. We walked up the grassy drive as we had been told to do and along the brick walk and into the schoolhouse.

Miss Effie sat in her captain's chair brushing the large gray cat which lay on a tall stool in front of her. We entered without speaking. Without looking up, Miss Effie said, "Now, young gentlemen, let's try that again—outside. Take off your caps before you step through the door, and say 'Good morning, ma'am' as you come through the door. Smile if you feel like it. Don't if you don't." She herself did not smile as we went out and came back in the manner she had suggested. However, this time she looked directly at us when she returned our "good mornings." Each child who entered in what she felt to be a rude way was sent out to try again.

Strangely enough she did not smile at anyone. She treated each child as an adult and each lesson as though it were a serious task. Even though there were occasional crying scenes or temper tantrums among us, she herself never lost her firm, rational approach. Sitting in her captain's chair, dressed in black from neck to toe except for a cameo, small gold loop earrings, and a gold and opal ring on her right hand, she was usually as solemn and considerate as a judge on his bench.

The third day she was again brushing the cat as we entered. She waited until we were all properly in before addressing us as a class. "This is Mr. Thomas. He's a no-good cat, and he doesn't like children, so leave him alone. I'd have nothing to do with him myself except that he happens to belong to me because his mother and grandmother belonged to me. They were no good either. But since he does belong to me and since he is here, we may as well talk about cats."

She showed us how to brush a cat, the spots under his neck where he liked to be rubbed, how he didn't like his ears or whiskers touched, how his ears turned to pick up sounds, how he stretched and shut his paw pads when he was tickled on the stomach or feet, and how he twitched his tail when annoyed. "Mr. Thomas is a fighter," she said—and she let us look at the scars from a dozen or more serious fights—"and he's getting too old to fight, but he hasn't got sense enough to know that."

She looked at us where we stood more or less in a large circle around her. "Now, let's see, I don't know your names. I know your mothers, but not your names." She would, she said, point to us one at a time and we were to give our names in clear, loud voices while looking her right in the eye. Then we were to choose a chair at one of the three tables.

"I hate the way most people become shy when they say their names. Be proud of it and speak up."

When the young ladies had finished giving their names, she said that they did admirably well; they chose to sit at the same table. One or two boys shouted their names in a silly fashion and had to repeat. One or two others looked away, to decide on a chair or to watch the cat, they claimed, and so had to repeat. I did not speak loud enough and had to say my name three times. One lad refused to say his name a second time, and that day and the next she called him Mr. No-Name. On Friday he did not appear, or Monday or Tuesday, and the next week a new boy from the waiting list gave his name in a perfect fashion and took Mr. No-Name's place.

We learned about cats and names the third day then. The following day Barbara Ware and Robert Barnes distinguished themselves by claiming to like their coffee black with no sugar, just the way Miss Effie was convinced it should be drunk.

At the end of the second week we reviewed what we had learned by sweeping and dusting the room again. And each day we practiced coming in and leaving properly and saying our names in a way that sounded as though we were proud of them and of ourselves—which by then we were.

The third week, putting down the cat brush and shooing Mr. Thomas off the stool, Miss Effie said that she too was proud of the way we identified ourselves with eyes level and unblinking. "But now," she said, "I want to teach you to give a name that is not your own—without any shiftiness."

She sat with both thin hands clasping the arms of her chair and gave a short lecture. Not everyone, she said, was entitled to know your name. Some people of a certain sort would ask when it was none of their business. It would be unnecessarily rude to tell them so. But we could simply tell such people a name that had nothing whatever to do with our own. She did not mention kidnappings, but talked rather about ruthless salesmen, strangers on buses and trains, and tramps and beggars wandering through the neighborhood.

For the purpose of practice, all of the young ladies would learn to give in a courteous, convincing manner the rather dated, unconvincing name "Polly Livingstone." The boys would be, when asked, "William Johnson" (a name I can still give with much more conviction than my own). That day and the next we each gave our own names before the coffee break, and after coffee, our false names. We liked the exercises in which we went up to her, shook her hand if she offered it, and gave our false names, confronting, without staring, her solemn gaze with ours. If we smiled or twisted, we had to stand by the fireplace until we could exercise more poise.

At the end of the first month Miss Effie said that she was fairly well pleased with our progress. "I have taught you, thus far, mainly about rooms. Most people spend most of their lives in rooms, and now you know about them."

She mentioned some of the things we had learned, like how to enter rooms: ladies first, young men bareheaded with their caps in their left hands, ready to offer their right hands to any extended, how to look a person directly in the eye and give one's name (real or false, depending on the occasion) without squirming, how to sweep and dust a room, and finally how to leave a room promptly, without lingering, but without running or giggling.

"What else have we learned about rooms?" she then asked, letting Mr. Thomas out the window onto the sunny ledge where he liked to sit.

"How to drink coffee," Miriam Wells said rather proudly.

"No," Miss Effie said, "that has to do with another series which includes how to accept things and how to get rid of things you don't want: fat meat, bones, seeds, pits, peelings, and"—she added under her breath—"parents." She paused for a moment and looked pleased, as though she might wink or smile, but her angular face did not change its expression very much. "No. Besides, I'm not pleased with the way you're drinking coffee." She then said for the first time a speech which she repeated so often that by the end of the year we sometimes shouted it in our play on the way home. "Coffee is a beverage to be enjoyed for its flavor. It is not a food to be enriched with milk and sugar. Only certain types of people try to gain nourishment from it. In general they are the ones, I suspect, who show their emotions in public." (We had, I'm sure, no idea what the speech meant.) She expected us by June—possibly by Christmas—to be drinking it black.

75

"Is there anything else we need to know about rooms?" she asked.

"How to build them," Phillip Pike said.

"That," Miss Effie said, "you can't learn from me. Unfortunately. I wish I knew."

She looked thoughtfully out the window to the ledge on which Mr. Thomas was grooming himself. "Windows!" she said. "How to clean windows."

Again the cupboard was opened, and by noon the next day we knew how to clean windows inside and out and how to adjust all the shades in a room to the same level.

When it turned cold in November—cold enough for the stove but not the fireplace—we settled down to the real work which had given Miss Effie's kindergarten its reputation: Reading. Miss Effie liked to read, and it was well known in the town and especially among the public school teachers that the two or three hundred children she had taught had grown up reading everything they could find. She assured us that even though we were only five years old we would be reading better than the third-grade schoolchildren by the end of the year.

Each morning the stove was already hot when we arrived. She would brush Mr. Thomas awhile; then when we were all in our places and warm, she would hand out our reading books, which we opened every day to the first page and laid flat before us on the tables. While we looked at the first page she began heating the big red enamel pot of coffee, and also, because we needed nourishment to keep warm, a black iron pot of oatmeal. Then Miss Effie would sit down, allow Mr. Thomas to jump into her lap, and begin reading—always from the first page in an excited tone. She would read to the point exactly where we had finished the day before, so that from necessity she read faster each day while we turned our pages, which we knew by heart, when we saw her ready to turn hers.

Then one after another we went up to her and sat on Mr. Thomas's stool by the stove and read aloud to her while those at the tables either listened, or read, or played with architectural blocks. The child on the stool was rewarded at the end of each sentence with two spoonfuls of oatmeal if he read well, one if not so well. Since we each read twice, once before coffee and once after, we did not really get hungry before we left the school at noon. Of course those who read fast and well ate more oatmeal than the others.

In addition to the reading lessons, which were the most important part of the day, we learned to take money and shopping lists to Mr. Zenacher's grocery store, to pay for groceries, and to bring them back with the change. Usually two or three of us went together to the store on the next block. At the same time three or four others might be learning to paint flowerpots or to catch frying-size chickens in the chicken yard back of the barn.

On sunny days that winter we would all go out to the greenhouse for an hour and learn to reset ferns and to start bulbs on wet beds of rock. In March we learned how to rake Miss Effie's tennis court, to fill in the holes with powdery sand, and to tie strings properly so that later a yardman could mark the lines with lime. The tennis court was for rent in the afternoons to high school girls and boys during the spring and summer.

By Eastertime we were all proficient sweepers, dusters, shoppers, bulb setters, readers, and black-coffee drinkers. Miss Effie herself, now that spring was almost in the air, hated to sit all morning by the stove where we'd been all winter. Usually after an hour or so of reading all aloud and at once, we would follow her into the yards and prune the first-breath-of-spring, the jessamines, the yellow bells, and the peach and pear trees. We kept the branches we cut off, and we stuck them in buckets of water in the greenhouse. Miss Effie printed a sign which said "Flowers for Sale," and we helped her tie it to a tree near the sidewalk. In addition to the flowering branches which we had forced, she sold ferns and the jonquils that we had set, which were now in bud.

All in all, spring was a busy time. And I remember only one other thing we learned. One warm May morning we arrived to find Mr. Thomas, badly torn about the ears, his eyes shut, his breathing noisy, on a folded rug near the open door of the schoolhouse. We wanted to pet him and talk to him, but Miss Effie, regarding him constantly, said no, that he had obviously been not only a bad cat but a foolish one. She believed he had been hit by a car while running from some dogs and that that was how the dogs got to him. (She and Miss Hattie had heard the fight during the night.) At any rate, he had managed to crawl under the steps where the dogs couldn't get to him anymore. At dawn she had come down and thrown hot water on the dogs and rescued him.

As soon as a boy from her cousin's office arrived (her cousin was a doctor) she was going to teach us how to put a cat to sleep, she said.

We pointed out that he already seemed to be asleep.

"But," she explained, not taking her eyes from the cat, "we are going to put him to sleep so that he won't wake up."

"You're going to kill him?" Robert Barnes said.

"You could say that."

We were all greatly disturbed when we understood that this was the last we would see of Mr. Thomas. But Miss Effie had no sympathy, apparently, for the cat or for us. "He is suffering, and even if he is a no-good cat, he shouldn't suffer."

When Barbara Ware began to whimper, Miss Effie said, "Animals are not people." Her tone was severe enough to stop Barbara from crying.

After the boy had arrived with the package and left, Miss Effie stopped her reading, went to the cupboard, and got out a canvas bag with a drawstring top. "Now if you young ladies will follow us, I'll ask the young gentlemen to bring Mr. Thomas."

We all rushed to be the ones to lift the piece of carpet and bear Mr. Thomas after her through the garden to the toolshed. "Just wrap the carpet around him. Tight. Head and all," she instructed when we reached the toolshed. After we had him wrapped securely, Miss Effie opened the package and read the label—"Chloroform." She explained to us the properties of the chemical while we rolled the cat tighter and stuck him, tail first, into the canvas bag. Miss Effie asked us to stand back and hold our breaths. She then soaked a large rag with the liquid and poured the rest directly onto the cat's head and on the carpet. She poked the rag into the rolled carpet so that it hid Mr. Thomas completely. She then drew the drawstring tight and placed the cat, bag and all, in the toolshed. She shut the door firmly and latched it. "That'll cut out the air," she said.

Back in the schoolhouse, we tried to listen as she read, without the usual excited tone, but we were all thinking about Mr. Thomas in the toolshed. "Well," she finally said, "if you will excuse me a moment, I'll go see if my cat is dead."

We watched from the windows as she walked with her cane through the garden to the toolshed. We could see her open the door and bend over the sack for a long time. At last she straightened up and locked the door again. She came back with the same unhalting gait and stood for a moment in the sun before the open door of the schoolhouse.

"When I dismiss you, you're to go straight down the drive and straight home. And if they want to know why you're home early"—she stopped and studied the ground as though she had lost there her cameo or her words—"tell them the only thing Miss Effie had to teach you today was how to kill a cat."

Without waiting for us to leave, she walked in her usual dignified fashion down the brick walk and up the back steps and into her house, shutting the kitchen door firmly behind her. I know that that was not the last day of school, for I remember helping to spread tablecloths over the reading tables, and I remember helping to serve teacakes to the mothers who came the last day and stood on the tennis court near the table where Miss Hattie was serving coffee. But the final, definite picture I have of Miss Effie is that of her coming through the garden from the toolshed and standing in the doorway a moment to say that she had nothing more to teach us.

THE BOX HOUSE
AND THE SNOW

Cristina Henríquez

Their house was a box. It was a perfect house. It was the father's favorite thing in the world. No one else he knew had a house quite like it and no one, he thought, ever would again. It was the sort of place that should go on the National Register of Best Houses, if such a thing existed. And if it didn't exist, it should be invented to honor this one house.

They lived in a valley between two mountains. There were forty-two other houses in their modest valley town. There were once forty-three other houses, but a few years earlier a whipping windstorm had its way with one of them and toppled it into a pile of matchsticks and glass. The man whose house had fallen had built the house himself, a feat he often boasted of at length to everyone in the town. So when it crumbled, though they were nothing but kind and supportive to his face, the people in the town whispered behind the man's back about how embarrassing it was that the house had collapsed like a bad soufflé, and they laughed with derision and agreed that the man's pridefulness had been met with just punishment. The father was among those whispering and laughing and agreeing, though it scared him to recognize a bit of himself in the man, since the father, too, was buoyed by pride. But when he confessed this fear to his wife, she assured him that there was a difference between arrogant pride and joyous pride, and that the father possessed the latter, which was the acceptable variety. The father felt better. He even hired a photographer to take a picture of him and his wife and their daughter in front of their perfect house, to commemorate his joyous pride.

The valley town was huddled in the middle of a tropical country. The people there were used to air that never dropped below eighty degrees, air that was sticky and warm every year of their lives. So they were more than a little surprised when, one April morning, they encountered a curious white substance covering nearly everything they could see. The substance was snow.

Later, this is the story they would collectively decide upon, the legend they would pass down to their children and their children's children: The snowstorm came at night while everyone was sleeping. The world was perfectly still. No breeze rustling the trees; no whispers ribboning through the air; no animals yawning; no people turning in their sleep, flinching from their dreams; no soft gurgling in the sewers below the streets. The moon was masked behind thick clouds. The world was black, caked on and opaque. Then, all at once, millions of snowflakes burst from the murky sky and fluttered to the earth. It was a pillow ripping open. It was a silent, exploding firework. It was as if God had been collecting mounds and fistfuls and armfuls of snow for centuries and, finally, could hold the white flakes no more. He tore a seam in the fabric of heaven and sent the snowflakes scampering forth. At first, the snow danced through the air doing cartwheels, doing flip-flops, doing triple full twists and Arabian front tucks. Later, carried by a new wind, it leapt in great tumbling clumps like paratroopers. As the night went on, it shot down in a nosedive, in a fury, as if thrust from the sky against its will, as if spit from the mouths of angels. And later still, in a last heroic push before the sun came up in the morning, the snow grew so dense that it gave the appearance of cascading walls of snow, a world made from snow, solid all the way through. There was so much of it that the entire night sky was blanched, and the earth below it surrendered. The world turned white.

But before the people in the valley town settled upon this story, they had to deal with the astonishment of that morning. When they first woke their shutters were closed, as they were every night, to block out the blinding morning sun. There was a chill in the air stiffer than usual, but not enough to provoke alarm. It was not until, one by one, the people climbed out of bed and opened their doors that they noticed the snow. People plunged into the waist-high sea of white that flooded into their doorways. They looked out from their houses for their neighbors, for trees, for wire trash cans, for street signs—for anything familiar—but found that only the top half of every-thing was visible. Against houses and buildings, the snow soared, swept up gently by the wind like a cresting wave frozen in time.

The phones were quiet.

The electricity was severed.

The sewers were frozen.

Inside their houses, people talked on and on and on among themselves, in complete disbelief, trying to comprehend the world outside their windows.

In the perfect house, the father was the first one awake. He found himself pressed against his wife when he opened his eyes. He was shivering. For a moment, he believed he was sick. He groped for his watch on the bedside table and held it in front of him but, because of the perfect darkness in the house, he could not see the face. For a moment, he believed he had gone blind. He curled his icy toes around his wife's ankle. He smoothed the standing hairs on his arms. He stared into pitch-blackness and then became scared. His wife's ankle was as cold as his toes. For a moment, he believed he was dead.

When finally he got up, the father pulled three pairs of socks over his feet and padded to the front door, stealing his way through the dark. The iciness of the wrought-iron door handle shocked him but when he opened the door, slowly, pulling it toward him, what he saw shocked him more: a bright white earth that stretched for miles. The snow that had built up against the door gently tumbled into the house. The father tried to nudge it out with his toe and in doing so, made a soft indentation at the bottom of the snow wall. He stared at the glittering snowscape. He took a step back into the house and closed the door.

The mother felt the cold slink in through her pores and spread like a vapor under her skin. In the night, she thought it was a dream. She pulled a sheet over her body and fought her way into a ball, holding her knees to her chest to stay bunched. She slept restlessly, trembling. She knew something was not right.

And then the father poked her in the morning. He whispered, Get up.

It's the middle of the night, she told him. It's dark.

It's not dark. It's just that the windows are covered.

Well then open the shutters. You always open the shutters when you get up.

The shutters are open.

What do you mean? the mother asked, sighing.

You'll see, the father said. He pulled her out of her ball.

What's going on? she asked.

The father slid socks over her feet as she sat on the bed. She was growing impatient.

You won't believe it, he told her. Then he dragged her through the house, guiding her with his hand.

I can't see a thing, she said.

The father opened the door for her. Light streamed into the house. He gave a dramatic bow. See this, he said.

The snow was big news. Reporters from all over were clamoring to cover it, but the problem was that they couldn't get into the town because the roads were blocked. The networks that could afford to sent helicopters to hover over the town. The shots were incomparable. The earth smoothed over, soft shimmering dimpled mounds. One network from Chile was so desperate to cover the story—which was being hailed as a miracle on par with tears from the statue of the Virgin Mary—that they diverted their traffic copter to the valley town. The result was sixty-six traffic accidents in Santiago in one day—a sort of anti-miracle.

The people in the town, eager to be on television, worked hard to clear pathways for the reporters to make their way in. They cleared streets using pots, pans, cookie sheets, watering cans, bowls, plastic bags, shoes, pillowcases, and couch cushions—

anything they could find. The work was hard. They weren't prepared. They safety-pinned towels around their thighs and around their torsos to help keep their bodies warm. They swirled blankets around their shoulders and clutched them at the front to keep them closed. They lit their stoves and took turns warming their reddened hands over the hissing blue flames. They picked up their phones for a dial tone—to call the stations and invite them in—but were greeted by silence on the other end. They pulled at their TV knobs, hoping to see themselves on the news, hoping to see a government emergency alert, but the TVs stayed asleep. They took photographs of the great white ocean that had swallowed them whole, forcing teeth-chattering smiles for the camera as they stood outside. Two enterprising families trampled on the snow, spelling out HOLA with their footprints, and this image, captured by the swarm of helicopters overhead, became the most famous of the miracle snow.

The father used a silver platter he and the mother had received for their wedding to push the snow aside, enough so he could walk out the door. The soles of his sandals stamped a pattern of diamonds on the white land as he walked. He stopped at his fence, an iron fence ornate with curlicues and swirls. Snow rested in the spaces of the design. The father poked his finger at the snow. It came loose like a cutout and fell quietly against the powder on the other side. But he had not ventured outside, as others had, for fun or novelty. The father turned and looked at his perfect house, ambushed by snow. He thought of the man whose house had blown down as punishment for his pride. The father told himself that if he could keep his house standing, it would be God's way of telling him he had a reasonable sort of pride, one for which he did not deserve to be punished. On the other hand, if something happened to the house, it would mean that the father was a sinner, since the wrong sort of pride was a sin. On top of that, there were the news cameras. If the house collapsed, almost everyone in the world would know it. Things were getting serious.

Inside, the father told the mother to gather dishrags and bath towels. The mother was sitting at the kitchen table with her knees pulled to her chest, trying to stay warm. She had checked on the daughter but let her keep sleeping. At this point, it seemed better than being awake. The mother raised her eyebrows as the father pointed to the wooden wall behind the sink.

Do you see how dark it is? he asked.

The mother turned to look. Something black blossomed in a patch above the sink.

It looks like a stain, she said.

It's water, the father said. It's seeping through.

But it rains here and the wood gets wet, the mother said.

The father shook his head. The snow is wrapped around the house like a boa constrictor. It's not the same as rain.

The mother was worried now but the father told her not to be. Get the dishrags and towels, he said. He showed her how to hold them up to the walls, how to use them to swab the water away.

The father woke the daughter next. Are you awake? he yelled. You have to get up! There's been a snowstorm, he said. He heard the daughter laugh from her room.

The father opened her bedroom door. It's true, he said.

But it doesn't snow here, the daughter argued.

I'm almost positive that's what it is. I've seen pictures before.

89

The daughter jumped up, giddy. Is it really? She rushed past the father to the front door. When she saw the snow, she shuddered and pulled her arms in through the sleeves of her nightgown. The air smelled like it had been laundered, fresh and wet. A bird sprang lightly into the snow, sinking in and flitting off again.

It's amazing, the daughter whispered.

Yes, okay, the father said, dragging her away from the door. That's enough of that. We need your help.

The father took a wooden chair from the kitchen and put it in what he estimated was the center of the house. Already the ceiling had begun to bow. The mother said she couldn't tell, but the father saw it. The roof was flat and the weight of the snow would collapse it.

The father told the daughter to put on her best socks and her warmest clothes. The mother, who could see what was coming next, protested. I'll stand on the chair myself, the mother said.

I've already taught you how to swab the walls, the father argued.

I'll teach the girl.

It will take too long. Someone needs to get on the chair now and that's the girl.

The mother bit her tongue.

The father told the daughter to stand on the chair.

No way, she said.

Do it or I'll bury you in that snow, the father shouted.

That's terrible, the mother said. Don't say that to her.

The father sighed. You're right. I'm feeling a little crazy. I'm sorry. *Please* get up on the chair.

The daughter put her arms back through her nightgown's armholes and climbed up wordlessly, her dark hair swimming down her back.

Reach your arms up, the father said. His expression was grave, his eyes wide and expectant.

The daughter did as he asked, gazing at the ceiling as her hands neared the wood.

Can you touch? the father asked.

The daughter flattened her palms against the ceiling.

The mother said, Are you okay?

The daughter said, I guess.

The father said, Now don't move.

Very slowly, small paths began to open up all over the town like arteries, allowing people to get around to most places, allowing life to flow again. The reporters gave round-the-clock updates and when by that evening not a single new snowflake had fallen, most of them packed up and left.

As far as the father knew, no one else's house had suffered. They all had sloped roofs so the snow tumbled off. For the first time, the father saw his own house as something less than perfect. It was not invincible. He complained about this to the mother.

But the mother said, This only proves it's *more* perfect than the rest. Because with this house comes a challenge. And surviving the challenge will only make you stronger. Do other people have houses that will make them stronger?

No, the father admitted, pleased by this logic. The father was also inspired by this logic. He went out and found one of the few news teams left in town and told them he had a knockout story for them. He promised them the greatest house in the world. The news team was about to leave the scene. There was only so much they could say about snow and only so much they could speculate about how it got there and what might happen next. But at the offer to see the greatest house in the world, they thought, Why not?

The news team arrived as the mother was squeezing rags over the sink. She was exhausted but the clay between the wood was softening so she had to work quickly. More than once, the mother had slumped in the corner and covered her face with one of the rags. She said a prayer, moving her lips against the terry cloth. She asked God to lift the snow, to suck it back into the sky. She imagined streamers of snow running up into the clouds. The dry earth would return to itself layer by layer.

The daughter stood, perched on the wooden kitchen chair in the middle of the floor, her arms spread and raised overhead, palms flat and pressed into the wet wood, fingers splayed. She watched her mother huddle in the corner. She heard whispering but could not make out the words. The daughter itched one ankle with the toes of her other foot. She wore red woolen knee-high socks that her mother had bought once to make into stockings for Christmas but never had. Then the daughter heard the commotion outside. Who's here? she said.

Who's where? the mother asked.

The daughter nodded her head toward the door.

The mother peered out and then shrieked.

At the sound of the shriek, the father looked up and strode to the house. Isn't it magnificent? he said, motioning toward the news team. Now everyone will know about our house. The whole world will be able to see it.

I'm not wearing any makeup, the mother said, and skittered to the bathroom.

The father peered outside at the crew and then looked to the daughter. Whatever you do, do not move, he said. Even after the snow melts, the wood will get heavy with water. You have to hold it up. The whole world will be watching.

The daughter sighed.

Don't sigh, the father scolded.

I don't think it will fall, the daughter said.

Do you really want to find out? the father asked.

Although the father had not foreseen it, the story ended up being not so much about the house as about the daughter standing inside the house, literally holding it together with her own two hands. The news team requested interviews with the daughter, but the father insisted that she not be bothered. She needed to focus. Sometimes, though, the daughter yelled out requests for food or pleas that someone trade places with her because she was growing tired, even though the father pinched her legs when she did because he didn't want her to make him seem like a cruel father in front of the whole world, as he kept saying.

Failing the opportunity to interview the daughter, the news anchor at least wanted to interview the father. The father welcomed the attention.

How much longer will the girl have to hold up the ceiling? the news anchor asked. She wore a pink suit. She was a gumdrop in the snow.

The snow has almost melted, the father replied.

Why can't we talk to her?

I already told you.

Tell me again.

If you start talking to her, she will be distracted. It's important for her to focus. She's holding up the most perfect house in the world.

Would a perfect house be capable of collapsing?

It won't collapse. You'll see.

Then the father flashed a huge smile at the camera, showing his gums.

Cut, the news anchor said.

Did you get a shot of the house? the father asked.

Sure, the news anchor replied.

When it was time for bed, the father told the daughter to stay on the chair.

All night? the daughter said. You have to be kidding.

All night, the father replied, and the daughter did as she was told.

The mother had trouble sleeping that first night. She kept dreaming she was wet. She kept feeling water edging under her skin, under her nails, into her ears. She would wake and touch her skin until she was sure it was dry, and then fall asleep, fitfully, again. She dreamed she was stuck underwater. She was submerged in a tank, floating in pale gray water. She was holding her breath but her lungs were losing air. She dreamed she was in the mouth of a volcano, buoyed by lava. She could feel the volcano rumbling beneath her. She could feel the vibrations traveling through her toes to her knees to her hips to her shoulders. And then the volcano exploded. She was thrown out. But what it spewed wasn't lava and ash. It was snow. And the mother landed face-down on the ground, snow raining over her. She tried to get up but she couldn't. The snow pushed her down like hundreds of tiny hands. She tried to open her mouth to scream but it was filled with the flakes. She dreamed she was choking on snow.

By the morning of the second day, the news team had grown bored even with the story of the girl. They packed up and left. The father learned this when he went out to bid them good morning. He was disappointed to see they had gone, but turned his attention again to the house. Conditions were better than yesterday. The sun was out and the father had managed to push the snow away from the house in a ring. The problem now was the rivulet of water surrounding the house. It would creep in at the baseboards, he knew. He would tell the mother where to concentrate her efforts today.

The daughter had been holding up the ceiling all night. Once, she bent her elbows the tiniest bit to see what would happen and she felt it: the ceiling began to give way. She restraightened her arms. She knew then that the father was right: If she got down, the ceiling would fall. The house would be ruined. Her shoulders popped. Her wrists creaked under the weight, warning her in a language of aching—*please, we won't be able to take it much longer*. But the daughter had no choice.

When the father came back inside, the daughter asked for breakfast. The father sped past her, spoke to the mother, and sped back out again, into town.

Hey, the daughter yelled after him, but the father seemed not to hear.

In certain parts of town, the snow was melting fast, trickling along the edges of itself, running into sewers and soil and lower land. One woman's sandals, which she had left on her stoop the night before the storm, were washed away by the runoff, gliding down the street into an open manhole. Armed with a flashlight, her husband was underground for hours, searching for her shoes.

By nightfall tomorrow, the townspeople guessed, the snow would be gone. When the earth had had enough, there would be flooding, but it had flooded before and they would handle it as they always had.

After the father left, the mother went out, too. The father had warned her repeatedly that one of them needed to stay at the house at all times to keep an eye on the daughter. And besides, the mother was supposed to be swabbing away. But the mother was restless and lonely in the house and when the father left, she wanted to go out, too.

I'll be gone for a little while, she told the daughter.

Can I come? the daughter asked.

The mother shook her head. I'll get you something if you'd like, she said.

I'm tired.

I know. It can't be much longer now.

I'm so tired.

The mother patted the top of the daughter's foot. Just hold on a little longer. I'll bring you a bag of marzipan.

The daughter was too exhausted to argue. Satisfied, the mother walked out the door, her feet crunching against the packed powder.

There was no telling how long the mother and father had been gone. But the daughter started to come undone. By now, the ceiling had lost almost all the snow, but the wood—saturated with water, soaked through by the unexpected winter—was nearly blackened and heavy with melting. The weight climbed into the daughter's bones. Her eyelids fluttered. She could no longer feel her hands. Her stockinged toes curled over the edge of the chair and her heels throbbed. Blood swelled in her neck and pooled in her shoulders. Her hips were cast forward, locked under the weight. It was as if the roof were fighting her, intent on crashing to the ground. She was beyond the point of crying out. She thought she couldn't do it. She thought it was too much. But she told herself: One more second now, one more second now, now it's just one more second. Fighting to keep herself going. And then, somewhere near the end of the day, the daughter started crying. Tears poured from her eyes the way the snow had gushed from the sky days earlier. Her entire body wept, sobbing with anguish.

When the father came back from town, he was relieved to see the house still intact. But he was unrelieved when he walked into the house. The daughter was still on the chair, her head lolling forward. The father hardly saw her. What he noticed instead was the water around his ankles. All over the floor. A calm layer, almost ten centimeters deep, filled the house from wall to wall. The father waded through it silently, the soft swish of water the only sound.

The mother came home then, too, and stood in the open door, water sliding out over her feet.

It's ruined, the father said softly. The water got through somehow. She let it through.

It could have come from anywhere, the mother said.

No. Everything around the house is dry. It came from the ceiling. I knew if it bowed enough, it would splinter. The water would come through.

The ceiling is still perfectly flat, the mother said, glancing up at it.

You could never see it, the father said. He knelt and lapped his hands through the water. It's ruined, he said again.

It will dry, the mother said.

The father shook his head. The ceiling will have to be rebuilt. The whole house.

If the father had raised his hands to his mouth, he would have tasted the salt of the daughter's tears, but he didn't. He simply scooped the water over and over with his hands, his back rounded, his head sinking farther into his chest.

Some books are damaged, the mother said. Only things on the floor!

It's the wood, the father said. It's too wet now. The walls are too soft. They'll fall in soon. She let it through, he whispered.

The daughter, her slender arms strained under the weight of the house, her tears long since dry, was too exhausted to speak. She simply stared at the father and held up the ceiling.

I JUST KEPT ON SMILING

Simon Burt

We were in class. It was my birthday. I was twelve.

I hadn't told anyone it was my birthday. I try not to tell anyone anything. But at breakfast Dom Gilbert, who hands out the mail, put two large envelopes by my plate, and wished me a Happy Birthday. Everyone at my table looked at me. Dom Gilbert waited, so I smiled at him, and he went away.

I opened them after breakfast. They were cards from home. One from my father and mother. One from my elder brother. I took the cards to the art room, where we're supposed to go every morning and fill our pens, and dropped them behind the press.

It was a Latin class. What we had to do was write sentences on the board. We all had a sheet of sentences, and Dom Francis sat at the back of the room and called out names. When your name was called you went up to the blackboard, and wrote your sentence on it in Latin. If you made a mistake the others were supposed to correct you. When Dom Francis was satisfied with your version, and this could take a long time, everyone copied it into his book, and you went back to your seat.

I took the books after I'd finished my sentence. I chose my moment carefully. While everyone was copying my sentence down, and Dom Francis was looking at his list to decide who was next, I took three exercise books from the pile on his desk. I took them back to my place, slipped them into my desk, and quickly wrote my sentence.

I sit at the front of the room. I prefer it that way.

At the end of the lesson Dom Francis collected in our books, and cleared his desk into his bag. Three was just the right number of exercise books to have taken. He wouldn't notice they were gone till he counted the pile.

After lunch we have half an hour to ourselves, before Games. We're meant to spend it in the day room. I like to spend it in the Chapel. If people ask where you've been, and you say the Chapel, they think you're a bit odd, but they don't say anything. The Chapel has a big gallery at the back where nobody ever sits except parents on Visitors' Day. I go there whenever I can, which isn't often, because I'm no fool. You can't keep a place if you go there too often. People nose you out. I go there once or twice a week maybe.

So after lunch I went back to the classroom, took the books from my desk, put them under my pullover—carefully, because I didn't want to crease them—and took them to the Chapel.

They were beautiful. Clean, stiff, and empty. When I opened them they crackled.

I held them by the edge. My hands are sweaty, and I didn't want to mark them.

I decided to keep them in the old vestment chest at the back of the gallery. It's full of old copes and chasubles and things that aren't used anymore. No one ever goes to it. It isn't even locked. I put the exercise books right at the bottom, and rearranged the vestments on top of them.

On the way down from the Chapel I met Nicky Carver. He said Hello, How are you, Happy Birthday. I smiled at him. I have a good smile. It makes people think twice.

Nicky Carver and I are about equal. He sits just behind me in class. His bed is opposite mine in the dormitory. We are about the same level in class. People usually bracket Nicky Carver and me together.

He walked with me to the changing room where we got ready for Games. I think he likes Games as little as I do, but there isn't any point in complaining.

The next time we saw Dom Francis was the last lesson before supper that evening. We all stood up when he came in, and said Good evening, Dom Francis. He said nothing.

He went to his desk and stood facing us. He looked at us all in turn. Behind me I could hear shifting feet. When it was my turn to be looked at I stared at the space between his eyes. He sat down.

I have bad news, he said. There is a thief among us. No one will sit down till he owns up.

I was still looking at the space between his eyes.

Well, he said. I'm waiting.

Nobody said anything.

This morning, he said, when I came to this class, I had twenty-seven exercise books. When I left I had twenty-four. Who can explain this?

He looked at us all in turn again. I looked at the bridge of his nose.

Very well, he said. I will give the thief a chance to redeem himself. My study will be open all tomorrow morning. I shall not be there. If, by twelve o'clock, the three exercise books are on my desk, I will consider the matter closed. Meanwhile, perhaps half an hour on your feet will improve your powers of concentration.

We stood for the rest of the lesson, and did Greek irregular verbs.

We had some time to ourselves again after supper. I spent it in the day room with Nicky Carver, playing chess. We discussed the rest of the class, and Nicky Carver tried to work out who had taken the exercise books. Nicky Carver is very religious. He has a brother in Rome, training to be a priest.

At lunch the next day Dom Francis rang the bell for silence and announced that he wanted to see all our class immediately afterwards in his study.

We formed a line outside his door, and Nicky Carver stood next to me.

When Dom Francis arrived he called us all in together and invited us to look at his desk.

As you can see, he said, the exercise books have not been returned. I must therefore punish the whole class.

Michael Byrne and Christopher Wynne-Wilson burst into tears. They often do.

What anyone, Dom Francis said, would want with three school exercise books is beyond me. I mean what possible use could there be for them? Be quiet, you two.

Michael Byrne and Christopher Wynne-Wilson managed to stop crying.

I apologize, Dom Francis said, in advance to those of you whom I must punish unjustly. To those of you who did not steal the books, and do not know who did. You must all understand that I have no choice. I shall see you all here at this time tomorrow, and I shall beat you all.

This time Anthony Forde joined Michael Byrne and Christopher Wynne-Wilson. Dom Francis looked at us as they cried.

Of course, he said, there is still time for the culprit to own up. And save his friends. I hope he does. Now go to Games.

After Games Anthony Forde, Timothy Pigott, and Freddy Oake came up to me in the changing room. Freddy Oake punched my arm. He often does.

Forde, he said, has got something to say to you. Tell him, Forde.

I saw you, Anthony Forde said. I saw you take them.

No, you didn't, I said. When was that?

At the end of the lesson, he said. Just before Dom Francis left. While he was collecting in our books. You leaned forward and took them off his desk.

So where are they now, I said.

Who knows? Freddy Oake said.

He punched my arm again.

And who cares? he said.

All we know, Timothy Pigott said, is that you're going to own up to Dom Francis.

They pushed me down onto the floor, Timothy Pigott sat on my chest and pulled my tie very tight round my throat.

You are going to tell Dom Francis, he said. Aren't you?

Yes, I said. Yes.

He let my tie go.

Aren't you? he said.

Yes, I said. I told you.

As I said before, I'm no fool. I know Timothy Pigott.

He got off my chest, and I sat up. They stood round me.

Just remember, Freddy Oake said. That's all.

Then they all kicked me, and went away. I finished changing.

After supper I went and spent some time in the Chapel. I didn't look at the exercise books. I didn't even go up into the gallery.

Nicky Carver came up to me in the dormitory that night.

I heard, he said. I don't think you should do it.

I smiled at him, but he didn't go away.

It's wrong, he said.

You know Pigott, I said.

So we all get beaten, he said. I don't think you should do it. It's wrong.

Never mind, I said. Quite a lot of things are wrong. Like taking the books in the first place.

It would be all right, he said, if you were doing it for us. But you're not. You're doing it because you're afraid of Pigott.

You bet I am, I said. Of course I am. Aren't you?

That's not the point, he said. I don't think you should do it.

We had Dom Francis again the second lesson next morning. We all stood behind our chairs. He sat down and told us to sit, and I stayed standing. He looked at me and I stared between his eyes.

The exercise books, I said. It was me. I took them.

Thank you, he said, for telling me. Come and see me at the end of the lesson.

He set us an unseen. I felt him looking at me about halfway through the lesson. I looked up and smiled, and he turned away.

After the others had left he called me up to his desk.

Well, he said. So it was you.

Yes sir, I said.

You are the thief, he said.

Yes sir, I said.

He sighed.

Who put you up to this? he said.

I don't know what you mean sir, I said. I'm owning up. I took them.

He brought his fist down hard on the desk.

Do you take me for a total fool? he said. Tell me who made you do this.

I'm sorry sir, I said. It's true. I did take them.

Then where are they? he said. Take me to them.

I didn't say anything.

Come on, he said. I'm waiting. Where are they?

I looked between his eyes, and then down at my feet.

I thought so, he said. Are you going to tell me who made you do it?

I'm sorry sir, I said. I don't know what you mean.

Get out, he said. Go away and tell your friends that they'll have to get up a lot earlier in the morning if they want to fool me. Go on. Get out.

Nicky Carver was waiting for me outside.

He didn't believe me, I said.

Good, he said.

At lunch Dom Francis rang the bell for silence again, and said we were all to see him in his study afterwards.

He stood us in rows in front of his table.

I'm sure you all know, he said, of this morning's disgraceful episode. So I will say no more about it. It has changed nothing. We must all resign ourselves to the knowledge that there is a thief in our midst. I don't know how he will live with his shame. He has stolen. He has betrayed his friends. There are parents, and members of staff, who are non-Catholics, or who have recently converted. What will they think of us now? You will all line up outside, and come in one by one for your punishment. Then you will wait outside till I dismiss you.

We lined up outside. I was near the end of the line. We counted eight strokes each. Michael Byrne and Christopher Wynne-Wilson cried. I was very careful not to look at Timothy Pigott. When it came to my turn, Dom Francis was red in the face and out of breath. His hair was all over the place.

I took down my trousers and bent over his chair and took my eight strokes. Dom Francis beats you with an old leather slipper.

Afterwards he held out his hand and I shook it.

You must see, he said, that I have no choice.

Yes sir, I said. Thank you sir.

When he'd beaten us all he called us all back in.

The incident is now closed, he said. I want you all to be very clear on this. Especially those of you who are responsible for this morning's misguided little charade, for which I have given you all two extra strokes. The matter will not be discussed again. I will punish any boy who does so.

Shame, I said to Nicky Carver as we were changing for Games. What does he know about shame?

We're not supposed to talk about it, Nicky Carver said.

I avoided Timothy Pigott as far as I could, in case his sense of honour was not as keen as Nicky Carver's. He left me alone. Perhaps two extra strokes were enough for him. Perhaps he didn't care now that it was all over. Anthony Forde tried to speak to me that night after supper, but I just smiled at him and looked away.

I didn't go to the Chapel for a week. I spent my free time in the day room with the rest. Sometimes I played chess with Nicky Carver. Most of the time I sat and read.

I thought of the exercise books often. How clean and white they were. How empty. Thinking about them helped me a lot. At the end of that week I went to the Chapel and looked at them. They smelled of incense from the vestments. I looked at them once or twice a week from then on.

I saw more of Nicky Carver. We went on walks together, and he told me about his home. He lives near Manchester. Exeat day came round, and his parents came down to visit him, and mine came to visit me. They met, and they talked, and we went out to tea.

His parents asked mine if I would like to go and stay with them during the holidays, and mine said that I would. They didn't ask me.

That evening I decided to tear up the exercise books and throw them away. I went to the Chapel after supper to get them, and took them to the lavatory. I tore them up into minute pieces and flushed them away. It took a long time. I thought I might keep a small piece to remind me of them but in the end I didn't.

I didn't need to be reminded of anything. I had a secret.

My mother wrote to me and said that she and Mrs. Carver had arranged that I was to spend a week with them after Easter. She was glad I had a friend, she said.

That evening I took Freddy Oake's tennis eyeshade, which I'd had my eye on for some time. He'd left it in the recess between the small Library and the second form classroom, and I took it after supper.

I went to the Chapel to inspect it, and sat looking at it for a long time. It was a cool crescent of shining green plastic. But it didn't have the magic of the exercise books. In fact I thought it might get in the way of their memory. So I decided to put it back.

I bumped into Nicky Carver on the way back to the recess. The eyeshade was under my pullover. He stayed with me and talked. About his home, and the woods near his home, where we'd walk when I came to stay. He came with me back to the small Library, and I slipped the eyeshade back into the recess.

He must have seen me do it. I caught him looking at me very oddly in the dormitory later. We were sitting up in our beds waiting for lights out. He just stared at me. I smiled at him, but he didn't stop. He just stared and stared till Dom Gilbert put out the light.

Before lunch the next day we were all lined up in the hall ready to go to lunch when Dom Francis came in to make an announcement. He called Nicky Carver out and told him to go and wait in his study. Then he spoke to us.

Some of you will remember, he said, that a few weeks ago we discovered that there was a thief among us. Not only a thief but a betrayer of his friends, as I was forced to beat his entire class because he would not own up. I said at the time that I did not know how he would live with his shame. And it seems that he cannot. He came to me this morning and confessed. You will all wait here, while I deal with him now.

Everyone stood very quiet. Dom Francis left the hall, and we all waited. I couldn't believe my ears. I could hardly breathe. I was furious. I bit my cheek I was so angry.

Dom Francis came back and told us we could go in to lunch. There was to be no talking.

Nicky Carver was standing on a table in the middle of the refectory. He was standing to attention, and there was a big placard round his neck saying, Thief.

We all went to our places and sat down. I was a server that day and had to help hand round the plates. We were all silent. When I'd finished handing round I sat down. It was so quiet

110

the noise of my chair scraping on the floor echoed round the room. I didn't want to eat. I stared at Nicky Carver and waited for him to look my way.

It took a long time but he did in the end. I smiled at him. He had stolen my secret. He looked away.

I carried on staring, and soon he looked back at me. I smiled again. I didn't eat anything. I just kept on smiling.

Mercedes Kane

Elizabeth McCracken

When she was a little girl in the 1940s, my mother read books about child prodigies and got jealous. She wanted to be one herself, but her memory worked in all the wrong ways. She remembered bus routes, birthdays, and the latest hairstyles; she forgot Latin, the *Moonlight Sonata*, and how a transistor works. You can't be a genius, she told me once, if you forget what it is you're geniusing, and if you're stupid, you might as well be absent-minded.

"No point in holding on to foolishness," she said.

She knew it didn't work that way, mourned what she forgot and despised what she remembered. Sometimes I caught her in the kitchen, singing along to one of my father's tapes of old rock and roll. She'd dance a little, or chop onions in time. Once I caught her standing stock-still in the middle of the room, both hands over her heart, like some crazy teen idol.

"Who knows why I remember all the words to *that*," she said, scowling at the Everly Brothers' voices like her memory was their fault. "A waste of brain space."

But words stayed with her like that; she had a good head for poetry, too. When I was small, she'd recite poems to me while I was in the bathtub, sometimes from books, sometimes from memory. Her favorites were by Mercedes Kane, one of her child prodigies from the forties, who wrote beautiful poetry at the age of eight—long fantasies about invented towns and country dirt roads, sonnets about famous painters. Mama first read about her in the *Register* when she was seven: they were the same age, and Mercedes Kane lived in Chicago, a few hours away. When Mama went to visit her Chicago cousins, she'd look around the streets, sure she'd recognize a girl genius. The *Register* said that Mercedes Kane could multiply five-digit numbers without even thinking, that she knew six real languages plus Esperanto, that she was a serious little girl, and quiet. We had a book of her poems; it was wrinkled with steam from my baths.

The Quiz Kids were on the radio around then, too, but my mother said they didn't interest her. "Show biz," she said to my father, who himself had been on a local kids show in Des Moines. He had won seventy-five silver dollars. One time, after they'd had a fight, my father snuck into my room and told me angrily: "She tried out for the Quiz Kids, and didn't get on. Sour grapes."

Still, Mama thought she had what it took, or could have had with the right attention. She blamed her parents, her mother in particular. "I was musical, I was mathematical," she said to Grandma Sarah one Thanksgiving. "I taught myself to read when I was four—you could've taught me even earlier."

Grandma just told her how bad it was to push children, and with eight kids, who had time, anyhow? Who knew which ones would be intelligent and which ones would be my Uncle Mark? Child prodigies were unhappy, she told Mama, they never got to play, they almost never did anything great when they were older. They got depressed; they committed suicide.

My mother didn't believe that. She was sure she would've been great in her twenties, thirties, forever, if she had just been encouraged to greatness early on. She wouldn't have gotten depressed—she was unfailingly, antagonistically pleasant. She was unlucky enough to be the only cheery member of her immediate family, and the only one without a sense of humor. She suffered around my father and me. If she was cheerful, we became angered by her cheerfulness and made gloomy jokes; if she tried to joke in return, we'd look at each other and roll our eyes. She was neat and organized; on vacations, my father and I wouldn't get out of our pajamas for days.

She divorced my father when I was eight. She couldn't divorce me. After the split, she taught French at a Catholic girls' school. She tried to teach me, too. It was impossible. She would've liked me better if I had been smart, but I wasn't.

"You were a lazy baby, Ruthie," she told me. How do you answer to that? She gave up on me, and dreamed of her own childhood, which had been happy. Her father was a quiet man who had loved everybody and died at forty-five, before we had a chance to meet. I never knew how to refer to him. Grandpa? Your father? Grandma Sarah's husband? She told me once that he would have asked me to call him Sidney, but calling a relative, an old man, a dead man, by his first name seemed impossible.

I was eleven when Mama found Mercedes Kane at the grocery-store lunch counter and brought her home. It was an astounding thing to do.

Saturday morning, I sat on the sofa in our apartment watching *Abbott and Costello Theater* on Channel 13. I watched it every week, had all the routines memorized.

Mama walked in, leading a strange woman by the hand.

"Ruthie, this is my friend Mercedes. She's going to stay with us awhile."

The name sounded familiar, but this woman—a friend? That had to be a lie. My mother's friends were as neat as she was and had names like Rita, Harriet, and Frances. This woman was small and puffy; she had long gray hair that was combed straight back and looked tangled. Her dress was a plain faded print; her feet were done up in men's slippers over several pairs of socks. And she was smoking: none of my mother's friends smoked.

My mother put her hand on the woman's shoulder and leaned down. "Would you like to take a bath, Mercedes?"

Mercedes shrugged my mother away. "Do I have to?"

I laughed, because she sounded just like me.

"Wouldn't you like to?"

"You're the hostess."

Mama led Mercedes down the hall to the linen closet. I knew she was taking one of the towels out, plumping it proudly. My mother bought expensive new towels every few months; it was a luxury she approved of.

I heard the bathroom door close, and Mama came back.

"Do you know who that is? Mercedes Kane! We have her poetry. This is *her*. I found her at Dahl's."

"The smart little girl?"

"That's her. She was sitting at the counter, eating a hamburger and smoking, and she was reading one of her own books—*The Rose in the Garden*, that's the one we have. I was having a cup of coffee, and I saw it, so I started to talk to her. I didn't know it was her, and she didn't say anything. She said her name was Mercedes, but she wouldn't tell me her last name. I asked her, you know, if she was the little girl I read about in the paper. 'Who?' she said. I said: math genius, language genius, girl who went to the University of Chicago when she was eleven? She said no. 'I used to write a little poetry,' she said."

"Maybe it's just somebody pretending to be her."

"No, I know it's her. I'm sure of it. So I invited her to stay here awhile."

"Doesn't she live somewhere?"

"She says she's got a room, but she won't say where." Mama sat down on the edge of our old chaise longue. "I can't believe it. Right here, Ruthie, Mercedes Kane. Now, don't mention what you know about her. She doesn't want to talk about it. She's just my friend, okay?"

"This is weird."

"It's okay, it's fine."

I'd never seen my mother so excited. She fussed around the living room, scratching her forehead, rubbing her chin. I think she was trying to look smart. Every now and then she stopped in the middle of the room, put her hands on her hips, and smiled. After a few minutes, she flipped off the TV.

"Hey," I said, although I had stopped watching it a few minutes before.

"Honestly, Ruthie. You'd think you didn't know how to read or write or walk around. There you are, every day, with your mouth open. Your brain will waste away."

"I'm not here every day. I don't watch that much."

"Any is too much."

"*Mama.*"

"Don't whine."

Mercedes came creeping in from the hall, wrapped in my mother's toweling robe. She was still smoking; it was like she didn't stop for a minute, not even for a bath. Even though her hair was wet, it didn't look clean. But her cheeks were bright pink—healthy pink—underneath all that tangle.

"You look much happier, Mercedes," my mother said. "Would you like a cup of coffee or tea?"

"A cup of black coffee, please." She bowed oddly from the waist. The bath had washed away her rudeness.

"Well, it was a fast bath, anyhow," said Mama. "Was it a good bath?"

"Yes, thank you. Nice big bathtub."

"That's true. Old-fashioned. They don't make them that deep anymore. Mercedes," my mother said. "You have just the prettiest coloring. A healthy glow, I'd call it."

"Yes, that's one thing." Mercedes squinted at the smoke at the end of her cigarette. "I can't ruin my health, no matter how hard I try."

That evening, when I walked into the kitchen, my mother was speaking French. Mercedes peered into her coffee cup, smiling and nodding. I could tell Mama was asking a question, but Mercedes didn't respond, and finally my mother rolled out one set of words several times, adding "Mercedes" in her fancy accent. Finally, in exasperation, in her regular voice, she said, "*Mercedes.*"

"Hmmm?"

My mother repeated her French question.

"Are you talking to me?"

"I have been, for the past five minutes."

"Oh, I wasn't paying attention. I thought you were talking on the phone."

"But I've been right here in front of you, honey. I'm all excited to really talk French with somebody, it's been so long."

Mercedes shrugged one shoulder and tilted her head. "I don't know any French."

"Oh, I'm sure you do," Mama said. "I mean, I remember reading—"

"That was someone else, I'm sure. All I know is English, and I'm not too handy with that."

"But I remember," said Mama. "The papers all those years ago. You spoke eight languages. You even made a language up."

"No." Mercedes frowned. "Somebody else."

"It wasn't," Mama insisted. "It was you, Mercedes. I remember."

"There were a lot of little girls in the news."

"I wouldn't forget. I wanted to be like you."

"Maybe one of the Dionne quints."

That made Mama laugh. "I wanted to be a quintuplet, too, but I figure I can't blame my parents for that. But you, you were a mathematician—"

"No. I can't even add. I've barely got a brain."

"But you wrote those poems, right? You admit that."

Mercedes rested her tongue on her lip, as if she were wondering whether an admission would taste good. "No," she said finally. "I'd like to be able to say I did . . ."

Mama leaned against the table, sighed, and watched Mercedes with one eye half-closed, the other one open as far as it would go. I recognized the look: It said, How-stupid-do-you-think-I-am-I-know-you-did-it. I got it when I broke something and blamed the air, and I got spanked. But Mama just shook her head now and said, "Let me take you out to dinner tonight. You and me and Ruthie. Anywhere you like. How about the Hotel Fort Des Moines? You can borrow one of my dresses if you want."

"How about Noah's for pizza?"

"Oh, for Pete's sake, Mercedes, I want to take you someplace nice, someplace we'll enjoy ourselves."

"I'll enjoy pizza," Mercedes said firmly.

"But—"

"I wouldn't like the Fort Des Moines. I hate the downtown."

"Pizza sounds good," I said from my spot near the door.

They turned and looked at me, surprised.

"There you go," said Mercedes.

"Pizza," said my mother. "Okay."

So we went to Noah's, where Mercedes drank cup of coffee after cup of coffee, Mama keeping pace with glasses of red wine. At the end of the meal, Mama stood up, held her purse to her belly with a fist, and asked Mercedes if she wouldn't mind driving.

"No problem," said Mercedes. She drove very carefully. In the garage at home, she got out and gave the hood of the car a pat.

"Never drove a standard before," she said. "Just a matter of coordination, isn't it?"

Mama went to bed right away. I sat in my room at my desk, drawing cartoons to amuse myself. I had an old Fred Astaire record on the player. It had been an inheritance from my father's parents, the only thing I had wanted from their house. I felt soothed every time I listened to it.

Mercedes came to the door and knocked on the frame. "Who's this singing?"

"Fred Astaire."

She looked serious for a minute. Then she said, "Oh," smiling. "You're too young to know who he is."

"I got it from my grandparents. It's my favorite."

"I'm old enough to know, and even I don't."

"I watch his movies on TV all the time. You seen them?"

"No. TV's a habit you have to get into. Never did." She scratched her elbow with the palm of her hand. "Ruthie, do you have a radio I can borrow? I like listening to the talk shows."

"All I have is a clock radio. Mom's got a portable."

"She's asleep. I don't want to bother her."

"Take the clock radio. Tomorrow's Sunday. I don't need it."

"Thanks." Mercedes took the radio off the nightstand and followed the cord to the wall. "Your mother's an interesting lady. Very bright."

"Guess so," I said, turning back to my cartoons.

"She knows what to think. Things don't just pop into her head, you know?" She paused. "What're you working on? Homework?"

"Nope. Nothing."

"Oh." She held the radio as if she were trying to figure it out. "Well, goodnight."

"Goodnight."

Mercedes slept on the sofa in the living room that night, and the night after that, and then Mama borrowed a rollaway from the neighbors. I got used to Mercedes pretty quickly, but Mama was transformed. I watched her buzz around the living room, emptying ashtrays, discovering candy wrappers stuffed under chair cushions, removing ink stains from upholstery, never complaining. She plainly loved Mercedes, and that surprised me, because my mother wasn't impetuous about anything, least of all love: until I was eighteen, she hugged me only if one of us was going on a trip, and then it was all business. I knew she loved me, of course, but it was a careful affection: regimented, proper. Looking back, I realize she had started loving Mercedes the first time she read *The Rose in the Garden*. It's not even

surprising that she brought Mercedes home: Mama had been
looking for her for thirty years.

My mother started cooking complicated breakfasts: waffles,
bacon, even tiny steaks. Mercedes was an amazing eater. She
ate every dish separately: first eggs, scraping the plate clean,
then bacon, and finally potatoes. She drank coffee constantly,
and I think she ate caffeine pills in between. She barely slept.
I heard the talk-show hosts chatting from the living room
all night, and sometimes, Mercedes talked back. "Are you
crazy?" she asked. "You must be nuts!" Sometimes at breakfast
she told us about the loonies that phoned in: the woman who
knew her parakeet understood algebra but just couldn't flap
his wings well enough to communicate solutions, the man
who was sure that God proved himself in ball-game scores. "O
America," she said one morning, piercing the yolk of her fried
egg with a fork.

After breakfast, Mama went to work, I went to school, and
Mercedes went someplace, she wouldn't say where. Mama
thought maybe she had a job, but I pictured her at the library,
reading magazines or encyclopedias or comic books.

The Thursday after Mercedes arrived, Mama decided she
was going to give us haircuts. She spread newspapers on the
kitchen floor and got out her scissors and combs.

"Mercedes first," she said. She had sent Mercedes to wash
her hair, and it was still tangled, of course, when she sat down
in the kitchen. Mama went at it with a comb. I was at the
kitchen table, writing a report on the Boston Tea Party. It was
due the next day, and I hadn't even gone to the library.

"You have such beautiful hair," Mama told Mercedes. "All
you have to do is take care of it."

"It's a bother."

"Just take care of it. Ruthie wouldn't take care of hers, and I had to cut it all off. Be careful, or I'll do it to you."

Mercedes twisted around at the waist. "Don't." She wrapped her fist around her wet hair.

"I was just kidding. Don't take everything so seriously."

Mercedes turned back carefully. "Just a trim. Just enough to keep it growing."

"You want me to set it, too? I could do it up in little pin curls. My sisters and I used to do each other's hair."

I found that hard to believe. When I saw my mother talk to my aunts, they whispered fiercely about my grandmother. They never smiled.

"Okay . . . curls?" Mercedes sounded dubious.

"A few curls."

Mercedes set her head back and closed her eyes.

"We used to have the cutest hairdos when we were little," said my mother. "You know what we set our hair with? Kotex! The kind that attaches to a belt? We thought it was funny, but really, it was just perfect. Sterile, just the right size, and with little handles to tie."

I always thought my mother told these stories to embarrass me. Now Mercedes frowned, her cheeks getting even pinker. She kept her eyes closed.

"You should see my prom picture," Mama said. "All curls, dyed red. My father's in it—he got dolled up in a suit, because he knew my mother would want a picture of the two of us together." My mother sighed. "I look at that picture, and at the picture of me and Pop at my wedding, and I think: God. There's the right sort of man. There's the man I should've gone home with—not my date, certainly not my husband. My father was kind and smart and a good dancer. Your father—" she shook the comb at me accusingly, "—can't dance a step."

"Don't blame me. Not everybody's father is perfect."

"Be polite—"

"Mine wasn't, either." Mercedes opened one eye, turned it toward me, and closed it again. Then she lit a cigarette without even looking.

"But he wasn't a bad man, right? He encouraged you." Mama started to cut a tangle free.

"He encouraged me."

"My father was gallant. That's the word for him, just gallant. He always knew when to tell us we looked pretty. He owned a woman's clothing store, and he brought us home dresses. He always knew which one would flatter and fit which daughter. He had a genius for people. But he was serious, too. He was a good reader."

"My father was serious," said Mercedes.

"Well, he'd have to be. He was a professor, right?"

Mercedes paused the way she always did when she thought she was going to be fooled into something. "Yes," she said finally. "He taught geography. To this day, I can't locate Italy on the map."

"Anyone can find Italy," I said. "Even I know Italy."

"Not me," said Mercedes.

Mama started snipping at the ends of the hair. "But he encouraged you, you said. He gave you compliments."

"Not really. He didn't insult me. I barely saw him; I dealt with my mother. She gave me all my education. My father was an academic. He was too far away from reality to be ambitious. My mother wanted to be famous."

Mama bit her lip and looked at the back of Mercedes' head, trying not to look too interested, not knowing what to do to keep Mercedes talking.

She didn't have to do anything; Mercedes went on by herself. "He never paid much attention to me. I thought he didn't care about girls at all. My mother once said to me, thank God she found my father, who didn't notice the fact that she wasn't feminine. But once . . . I was sitting with him in his den, typing a paper. I loved typing, still do: if you work hard enough at it, you can be perfect, no mistakes—very satisfying. My father was sitting in his easy chair, reading a book. For some reason I mentioned my cousin Edith in St. Louis. My father looked up; whatever he was about to say was important enough to make him put down his book. 'Now, there's a pretty girl,' he said. 'Stunning, I'd say. Just beautiful. Always has been.' And there I was, just looking at my father. Slack-jawed. Cheated. All those years, pretending it didn't matter. How could he do that to my mother and me? He changed the rules right then, he just changed the rules."

We were quiet. Mama snipped awhile. "You're pretty," she said suddenly. "Mercedes, you're a very pretty lady."

"Mmmm," she said, her eyes still closed. "That's a lie. I mean, it's not like I ever wanted to be. I knew I was no good at it. I could look at Edith and see there was no point even thinking about it. I always wanted to be good at something, the best, so good that other people'd despair at even trying. But there never was anything."

"Very pretty," said my mother, "Beautiful hair, and color—"

"It doesn't matter, anyhow," I said.

Mercedes sat at attention and pointed at me. Her hair pulled out of my mother's fingers. "Bingo," she said. "That's it exactly." She stood up. "Enough. You're finished, aren't you?"

"I thought we were going to set it," said my mother.

"That's silly. A waste of time." Mercedes slipped off the towel that was around her neck and put it on the table. She looked embarrassed. "I'm going to rest."

"Well," said Mama. "I guess you're next, Ruthie."

"Can't we do it tomorrow? I have homework."

"Is it math? Mercedes can help you."

"No I can't," said Mercedes. "I haven't got a head for figures." She left the room, trailing smoke.

"Imagine," said my mother, after a moment. "Do you think that's it? Do you think that's what's done it? She's a genius, a genius, and all those years, just wanting to be pretty. She was famous, she was in the papers. Her future was so bright—"

"I don't think that's it," I said, but what I thought was: answers don't come that easy.

I woke up in the middle of the night, not knowing what time it was. Mercedes still had my radio. I walked to the kitchen to look at the clock and maybe get something to eat.

When I got there, Mercedes was at the table, reading my report where I had left it.

"Hey," I said crossly. I was sleepy and feeling fussy.

"Oh—" She dropped it. "I was just reading—"

"Well, don't. I don't need someone going through, correcting my spelling."

"I wasn't, I wouldn't." She stuttered, panicked. "I was only interested. I don't know anything about the Boston Tea Party."

I took the report off the table and crunched it up angrily. "I know I'm not smart. I don't need someone pointing it out. We all *know* you're a genius, Mercedes."

She looked terrified, as if I was going to hit her or make her speak French. "I'm not," she said. "I'm not at all smart. Please don't think I am."

"I don't know who you think you're fooling. I think it's mean pretending you're stupid when you're not. It's like pretending you're blind or crippled just to get out of stuff."

"Ruthie, Ruthie," she said. "You're smarter than you know."

"Mmmm," I said, doing a dead-on, cruel impression. "That's a lie."

We looked at each other. I shook my head and said, just like mother did sometimes, "You know, I simply don't understand you." It was true. I'm sure she heard it in my voice.

"Oh yes," she said. "That much I do know."

That night I cried in bed, replaying the scene. I was furious with myself, and furious with my mother, and furious with Mercedes. But I knew which one of us was guiltiest, and pinched my thighs and slapped my stomach, rolling in the sheets.

Mercedes disappeared before we got up. Mama was frantic— she took the day off work and drove around the city.

"Did she say anything to you?" she asked me. "Did she give you any hints?"

"No," I said, miserable. "Nothing."

I found a gift from Mercedes on my desk. It was my report, typed neatly, all the spelling and historical mistakes corrected, but without too much ambition. She had read and memorized it all at once—Mama said that she had a photographic memory. Mercedes knew that I wouldn't be too proud to take it if she snuck it in. I was grateful, I admit. I had ruined my only clean copy of it.

She left my mother a copy of *The Rose in the Garden*, with the word *Love* written on the title page. She didn't get around to signing her name. All there was was that one word.

We never heard from her again. Mama scouted the libraries, the grocery stores, the boarding houses. She took out classified ads in the newspapers, hoping that someone would find her and call us. Whenever we were in the car, looking down driveways and in doorways, if we spotted a small silhouette or a wisp of smoke, my mother slowed down. "That her?" she asked. I always was the one to decide it wasn't. At Christmastime, when she figured that Mercedes would be loneliest, Mama stuck up signs all over downtown that said, "Mercedes, We Miss You. Come Back For X-Mas. Love, Ellen and Ruthie." Nothing in return.

I turned in that report she wrote for me and got an F. The note at the bottom said: "You know you weren't supposed to get help."

SANDRA STREET

Michael Anthony

Mr. Blades, the new teacher, was delighted with the compositions we wrote about Sandra Street. He read some aloud to the class. He seemed particularly pleased when he read what was written by one of the boys from the other side of the town.

"Sandra Street is dull and uninteresting," the boy wrote. "For one half of its length there are a few houses and a private school (which we go to) but the other half is nothing but a wilderness of big trees." Mr. Blades smiled from the corners of his mouth and looked at those of us who belonged to Sandra Street. "In fact," the boy wrote, "*it* is the only street in our town that has big trees, and I do not think it is a part of our town at all because it is so far and so different from our other streets."

The boy went on to speak of the gay attractions on the other side of the town, some of which, he said, Sandra Street could never dream to have. In his street, for instance, there was the savannah where they played football and cricket, but the boys of Sandra Street had to play their cricket in the road. And to the amusement of Mr. Blades, who also came from the other side of the town, he described Sandra Street as a silly little girl who ran away to the bushes to hide herself.

Everyone laughed except the few of us from Sandra Street, and I knew what was going to happen when school was dismissed, although Mr. Blades said it was all a joke and in fact Sandra Street was very fine. I did not know whether he meant this or not, for he seemed very much amused and I felt this was because he came from the other side of the town.

He read out a few more of the compositions. Some of them said very nice things about Sandra Street, but those were the ones written by ourselves. Mr. Blades seemed delighted about these, too, and I felt he was trying to appease us when he said that they showed up new aspects of the beauty of Sandra Street. There were only a few of us who were appeased, though, and he noticed this and said all right, next Tuesday we'll write about the other side of the town. This brought fiendish laughter from some of us from Sandra Street, and judging from the looks on the faces of those from the other side of the town, I knew what would happen next Tuesday, too, when school was dismissed. And I felt that whatever happened it wasn't going to make any difference to our side or to the other side of the town.

Yet the boy's composition was very truthful. Sandra Street was so different from the other streets beyond. Indeed, it came from the very quiet fringes and ran straight up to the forests. As it left the town there were a few houses and shops along it, and then the school, and after that there were not many more houses, and the big trees started from there until the road trailed off to the river that bordered the forests. During the day all would be very quiet except perhaps for the voice of one neighbour calling to another, and if some evenings brought excitement to the schoolyard, these did very little to disturb the calmness of Sandra Street.

Nor did the steel band gently humming from the other side of the town. I had to remember the steel band because although I liked to hear it I had to put into my composition that it was very bad. We had no steel bands in Sandra Street, and I thought I could say that this was because we were decent, cultured folk, and did not like the horrible noises of steel bands.

I sat in class recalling the boy's composition again. Outside the window I could see the women coming out of the shops. They hardly passed each other without stopping to talk, and this made me laugh. For that was exactly what the boy had written—that they could not pass without stopping to talk, as if they had something to talk about.

I wondered what they talked about. I did not know. What I did know was that they never seemed to leave Sandra Street to go into the town. Maybe they were independent of the town! I chuckled a triumphant little chuckle because this, too, would be good to put into my composition next Tuesday.

Dreamingly I gazed out of the window. I noticed how Sandra Street stood away from the profusion of houses. Indeed, it did not seem to belong to the town at all. It stood off, not proudly, but sadly, as if it wanted peace and rest. I felt all filled up inside. Not because of the town in the distance but because of this strange little road. It was funny, the things the boy had written; he had written in anger what I thought of now in joy. He had spoken of the pleasures and palaces on the other side of the town. He had said why they were his home sweet home. As I looked at Sandra Street, I, too, knew why it was my home sweet home. It was dull and uninteresting to him but it meant so much to me. It was. . . .

"Oh!" I started, as the hand rested on my shoulder.

"It's recess," said Mr. Blades.

"Oh! . . . yes, sir." The class was surging out to the playground. I didn't seem to have heard a sound before.

Mr. Blades looked at me and smiled. "What are you thinking of?" he said.

He seemed to be looking inside me. Inside my very mind. I stammered out a few words which, even if they were clear, would not have meant anything. I stopped. He was still smiling quietly at me. "You are the boy from Sandra Street?" he said.

"Yes, sir."

"I thought so," he said.

What happened on the following Tuesday after school was a lot worse than what had ever happened before, and it was a mystery how the neighbours did not complain or Mr. Blades did not get to hear of it. We turned out to school the next morning as if all had been peaceful, and truly, there was no sign of the battle, save the little bruises which were easy to explain away.

We kept getting compositions to write. Mr. Blades was always anxious to judge what we wrote but none gave him as much delight as those we had written about Sandra Street. He had said that he knew the other side of the town very well and no one could fool him about that, but if any boy wrote anything about Sandra Street he would have to prove it. And when he had said that, he had looked at me and I was very embarrassed. I had turned my eyes away, and he had said that when the mango season came he would see the boy who didn't speak the truth about Sandra Street.

Since that day I was very shy of Mr. Blades, and whenever I saw him walking towards me I turned in another direction. At such times there would always be a faint smile at the corners of his mouth.

I stood looking out of the school window one day thinking about this and about the compositions when again I felt a light touch and jumped.

"Looking out?" Mr. Blades said.

"Yes, sir."

He stood there over me and I did not know if he was looking down at me or looking outside, and presently he spoke, "Hot, eh?"

"Yes," I said.

He moved in beside me and we both stood there looking out of the window. It was just about noon and the sun was blazing down on Sandra Street. The houses stood there tall and rather sombre-looking, and there seemed to be no movement about save for the fowls lying in the shadows of the houses. As I watched this a certain sadness came over me and I looked over the houses across to the hills. Suddenly my heart leapt and I turned to Mr. Blades, but I changed my mind and did not speak. He had hardly noticed that I looked up at him. I saw his face looking sad as his eyes wandered about the houses. I felt self-conscious as he looked at the houses for they no longer were new and the paint had been washed off them by the rains and they had not been repainted. Then, too, there were no gates and no fences around them as there were in the towns, and sometimes, with a great flurry, a hen would scamper from under one house to another leaving dust behind in the hot sun.

I looked at Mr. Blades. He was smiling faintly. He saw me looking at him. "Fowls," he said.

"There are no gates," I apologized.

"No, there are no gates." And he laughed softly to himself.

"Because . . ." I had to stop. I did not know why there were no gates.

"Because you did not notice that before."

"I noticed that before," I said.

Looking sharply at me he raised his brows and said slowly: "You noticed that before. Did you put that in your composition? You are the boy from Sandra Street, are you not?"

"There are more from Sandra Street."

"Did you notice the cedar grove at the top?" he went on. "You spoke of the steel band at the other side of the town. Did you speak of the river? Did you notice the hills?"

"Yes."

"Yes?" His voice was now stern and acid. His eyes seemed to be burning up from within.

"You noticed all this and you wrote about Sandra Street without mentioning it, eh? How many marks did I give you?"

"Forty-five."

He looked surprised. "I gave you forty-five for writing about the noises and about the dirty trams of the town? Look!" he pointed, "Do you see?"

"Mango blossoms," I said, and I felt like crying out: *"I wanted to show it to you!"*

"Did you write about it?"

"No." I just wanted to break out and run away from him. He bent down to me. His face looked harder now, though kind, but I could see there was fury inside him.

"There is something like observation, Steve," he said. *"Observation.* You live in Sandra Street, yet Kenneth writes a composition on your own place better than you."

"He said Sandra Street was soppy," I cried.

"Of course he said it was soppy. It was to his purpose. He comes from the other side of the town. What's he got to write on—gaudy houses with gates like prisons around them? High walls cramping the imagination? The milling crowd with faces impersonal as stone, hurrying on buses, hurrying off trams? Could he write about that? He said Sandra Street was soppy. Okay, did you prove it wasn't so? Where is your school and his, for instance?"

I was a little alarmed. Funny how I did not think of that point before. "Here," I said. "In Sandra Street."

"Did you mention that?"

Mercifully, as he was talking, the school bell sounded. The fowls, startled, ran out into the hot sun across the road. The dust rose, and above the dust, above the houses, the yellow of mango blossom caught my eye.

"The bell, sir."

"Yes, the bell's gone. What's it now—Geography?"

"Yes, sir," I said. And as I turned away he was still standing there, looking out into the road.

It was long before any such thing happened again. Though often when it was dry and hot I stood at the window looking out. I watched the freedom of the fowls among the tall houses, and sometimes the women talked to each other through the windows and smiled. I noticed, too, the hills, which were now streaked with the blossoms of the poui, and exultantly I wondered how many people observed this and knew it was a sign of the rains. None of the mango blossoms could be seen now, for they had already turned into fruit, and I knew how profuse they were because I had been to the hills.

I chuckled to myself. *There is something like observation, Steve.* And how I wished Mr. Blades would come to the window again so I could tell him what lay among the mango trees in the hills.

I knew that he was not angry with me. I realized that he was never angry with any boy because of the parts the boy came from. We grew to like him, for he was very cheerful, though mostly he seemed dreamy and thoughtful. That is, except at composition time.

He really came to life then. His eyes would gleam as he read our compositions and whenever he came to a word he did not like he would frown and say any boy was a sissy to use such a word. And if a composition pleased him he would praise the boy and be especially cheerful with him and the boy would be proud and the rest of us would be jealous and hate him.

I was often jealous. Mr. Blades had a passion for compositions, and I was anxious to please him to make up for that day at the window. I was anxious to show him how much I observed and often I noted new things and put them into my compositions. And whenever I said something wonderful I knew it because of the way Mr. Blades would look at me, and sometimes he would take me aside and talk to me. But many weeks ran out before we spoke at the window again.

I did not start this time because I had been expecting him. I had been watching him from the corners of my eyes.

"The sun's coming out again," he said.

"It's cloudy," I said.

The rains had ceased but there were still great patches of dark cloud in the sky. When the wind blew they moved slowly and cumbersomely, but if the sun was free of one cloud there would soon be another. The sun was shining brightly now, although there was still a slight drizzle of rain, and I could smell the steam rising from the hot pitch and from the galvanized roofs.

"Rain falling sun shining," Mr. Blades said. And I remembered that they said at such times the Devil fought his wife, but when Mr. Blades pressed me to tell what I was laughing at I laughed still more and would not say. Then thoughtfully he said, "You think they're all right?"

"What, sir?"

"In the 'mortelle root."

I was astonished. I put my hands to my mouth. How did he know?

He smiled down at me: "You won't be able to jump over now." And the whole thing came back. I could not help laughing. I had put into my composition how I had gone into the hills on a Sunday evening, and how the mango trees were laden with small mangoes, some full, and how there were banana trees among the immortelle and poui. I had written, too, about the bunch of green bananas I had placed to ripen in the immortelle roots and how afterwards I had jumped across the river to the other bank.

"They're all right," I said, and I pretended to be watching the steam rising from the hot pitch.

"I like bananas," said Mr. Blades. I was sure that he licked his lips as he looked towards the hills.

I was touched. I felt as one with him. I liked bananas, too, and they always made me lick my lips. I thought now of the whole bunch which must be yellow by now inside the immortelle roots.

"Sir . . ." I said to him, hesitating. Then I took the wild chance. And when he answered, a feeling of extreme happiness swept over me.

I remember that evening as turning out bright, almost blinding. The winds had pushed away the heavy clouds, and the only evidence of the rains was the little puddles along Sandra Street. I remember the hills as being strange in an enchanted sort of way, and I felt that part of the enchantment came from Mr. Blades being with me. We watched the leaves of the cocoa gleaming with the moisture of the rains, and Mr. Blades confessed he never thought there was so much cocoa in the hills. We watched the cyp, too, profuse among the laden mango trees, and the redness of their rain-picked flowers was the redness of blood.

We came to the immortelle tree where I had hidden the bananas. I watched to see if Mr. Blades licked his lips but he did not. He wasn't even watching.

"Sir," I said in happy surprise, after removing the covering of trash from the bunch. Mr. Blades was gazing across the trees. I raised my eyes. Not far below, Sandra Street swept by, bathed in light.

"The bananas, sir," I said.

"*Bananas!*" he cried, despairingly. "Bananas are all you see around you, Steve?"

I was puzzled. I thought it was for bananas that we had come to the hills.

"Good heavens!" he said with bitterness. "To think that you instead of Kenneth should belong to Sandra Street."

DAY OF THE BUTTERFLY

Alice Munro

I do not remember when Myra Sayla came to town, though she must have been in our class at school for two or three years. I start remembering her in the last year, when her little brother Jimmy Sayla was in Grade One. Jimmy Sayla was not used to going to the bathroom by himself and he would have to come to the Grade Six door and ask for Myra and she would take him downstairs. Quite often he would not get to Myra in time and there would be a big dark stain on his little button-on cotton pants. Then Myra had to come and ask the teacher: "Please may I take my brother home, he has wet himself?"

That was what she said the first time and everybody in the front seats heard her—though Myra's voice was the lightest singsong—and there was a muted giggling which alerted the rest of the class. Our teacher, a cold gentle girl who wore glasses with thin gold rims and in the stiff solicitude of certain poses resembled a giraffe, wrote something on a piece of paper and showed it to Myra. And Myra recited uncertainly: "My brother has had an accident, please, teacher."

143

Everybody knew of Jimmy Sayla's shame and at recess (if he
was not being kept in, as he often was, for doing something
he shouldn't in school) he did not dare go out on the school
grounds, where the other little boys, and some bigger ones,
were waiting to chase him and corner him against the back
fence and thrash him with tree branches. He had to stay with
Myra. But at our school there were two sides, the Boys' Side
and the Girls' Side, and it was believed that if you so much as
stepped on the side that was not your own you might easily get
the strap. Jimmy could not go out on the Girls' Side and Myra
could not go out on the Boys' Side, and no one was allowed to
stay in the school unless it was raining or snowing. So Myra
and Jimmy spent every recess standing in the little back porch
between the two sides. Perhaps they watched the baseball
games, the tag and skipping and building of leaf houses in the
fall and snow forts in the winter; perhaps they did not watch at
all. Whenever you happened to look at them their heads were
slightly bent, their narrow bodies hunched in, quite still. They
had long smooth oval faces, melancholy and discreet—dark,
oily, shining hair. The little boy's was long, clipped at home,
and Myra's was worn in heavy braids coiled on top of her head
so that she looked, from a distance, as if she was wearing a
turban too big for her. Over their dark eyes the lids were never
fully raised; they had a weary look. But it was more than that.
They were like children in a medieval painting, they were like
small figures carved of wood, for worship or magic, with faces
smooth and aged, and meekly, cryptically uncommunicative.

Most of the teachers at our school had been teaching for a long
time and at recess they would disappear into the teachers' room
and not bother us. But our own teacher, the young woman of

the fragile gold-rimmed glasses, was apt to watch us from a window and sometimes come out, looking brisk and uncomfortable, to stop a fight among the little girls or start a running game among the big ones, who had been huddled together playing Truth or Secrets. One day she came out and called, "Girls in Grade Six, I want to talk to you!" She smiled persuasively, earnestly, and with dreadful unease, showing fine gold rims around her teeth. She said, "There is a girl in Grade Six called Myra Sayla. She *is* in your grade, isn't she?"

We mumbled. But there was a coo from Gladys Healey. "Yes, Miss Darling!"

"Well, why is she never playing with the rest of you? Every day I see her standing in the back porch, never playing. Do you think she looks very happy standing back there? Do you think you would be very happy, if *you* were left back there?"

Nobody answered; we faced Miss Darling, all respectful, self-possessed, and bored with the unreality of her question. Then Gladys said, "Myra can't come out with us, Miss Darling. Myra has to look after her little brother!"

"Oh," said Miss Darling dubiously. "Well you ought to try to be nicer to her anyway. Don't you think so? Don't you? You will try to be nicer, won't you? I *know* you will." Poor Miss Darling! Her campaigns were soon confused, her persuasions turned to bleating and uncertain pleas.

When she had gone Gladys Healey said softly, "You will try to be nicer, won't you? I *know* you will!" and then drawing her lip back over her big teeth she yelled exuberantly, "I don't care if it rains or freezes." She went through the whole verse and ended it with a spectacular twirl of her Royal Stuart tartan skirt. Mr. Healey ran a Dry Goods and Ladies' Wear, and his daughter's leadership in our class was partly due to her flashing plaid skirts and organdie blouses and velvet jackets with brass buttons, but also to her early-maturing bust and the fine brutal force of her personality. Now we all began to imitate Miss Darling.

We had not paid much attention to Myra before this. But now a game was developed; it started with saying, "Let's be nice to Myra!" Then we would walk up to her in formal groups of three or four and at a signal, say together, "Hel-lo Myra, Hello *My*-ra!" and follow up with something like, "What do you wash your hair in, Myra, it's so nice and shiny, My-ra." "Oh she washes it in cod-liver oil, don't you, Myra, she washes it in cod-liver oil, can't you smell it?"

And to tell the truth there was a smell about Myra, but it was a rotten-sweetish smell as of bad fruit. That was what the Saylas did, kept a little fruit store. Her father sat all day on a stool by the window, with his shirt open over his swelling stomach and tufts of black hair showing around his belly button; he chewed garlic. But if you went into the store it was Mrs. Sayla who came to wait on you, appearing silently between the limp print curtains hung across the back of the store. Her hair was crimped in black waves and she smiled with her full lips held together, stretched as far as they would go; she told you the price in a little rapping voice, daring you to challenge her and, when you did not, handed you the bag of fruit with open mockery in her eyes.

One morning in the winter I was walking up the school hill very early; a neighbour had given me a ride into town. I lived about half a mile out of town, on a farm, and I should not have been going to the town school at all, but to a country school nearby where there were half a dozen pupils and a teacher a little demented since her change of life. But my mother, who was an ambitious woman, had prevailed on the town trustees to accept me and my father to pay the extra tuition, and I went to school in town. I was the only one in the class who carried a lunch pail and ate peanut-butter sandwiches in the high, bare, mustard-coloured cloakroom, the only one who had to wear rubber boots in the spring, when the roads were heavy with mud. I felt a little danger, on account of this; but I could not tell exactly what it was.

I saw Myra and Jimmy ahead of me on the hill; they always went to school very early—sometimes so early that they had to stand outside waiting for the janitor to open the door. They were walking slowly, and now and then Myra half turned around. I had often loitered in that way, wanting to walk with some important girl who was behind me, and not quite daring to stop and wait. Now it occurred to me that Myra might be doing this with me. I did not know what to do. I could not afford to be seen walking with her, and I did not even want to—but, on the other hand, the flattery of those humble, hopeful turnings was not lost on me. A role was shaping for me that I could not resist playing. I felt a great pleasurable rush of self-conscious benevolence; before I thought what I was doing I called, "Myra! Hey, Myra, wait up, I got some Cracker Jack!" and I quickened my pace as she stopped.

Myra waited, but she did not look at me; she waited in the withdrawn and rigid attitude with which she always met us. Perhaps she thought I was playing a trick on her, perhaps she expected me to run past and throw an empty Cracker Jack box in her face. And I opened the box and held it out to her. She took a little. Jimmy ducked behind her coat and would not take any when I offered the box to him.

"He's shy," I said reassuringly. "A lot of little kids are shy like that. He'll probably grow out of it."

"Yes," said Myra.

"I have a brother four," I said. "He's awfully shy." He wasn't. "Have some more Cracker Jack," I said. "I used to eat Cracker Jack all the time but I don't anymore. I think it's bad for your complexion."

There was a silence.

"Do you like Art?" said Myra faintly.

"No. I like Social Studies and Spelling and Health."

"I like Art and Arithmetic." Myra could add and multiply in her head faster than anyone else in the class.

"I wish I was as good as you. In Arithmetic," I said, and felt magnanimous.

"But I am no good at Spelling," said Myra. "I make the most mistakes, I'll fail maybe." She did not sound unhappy about this, but pleased to have such a thing to say. She kept her head turned away from me, staring at the dirty snowbanks along Victoria Street, and as she talked she made a sound as if she was wetting her lips with her tongue.

"You won't fail," I said. "You are too good in Arithmetic. What are you going to be when you grow up?"

She looked bewildered. "I will help my mother," she said. "And work in the store."

"Well I am going to be an airplane hostess," I said. "But don't mention it to anybody. I haven't told many people."

"No, I won't," said Myra. "Do you read *Steve Canyon* in the paper?"

"Yes." It was queer to think that Myra, too, read the comics, or that she did anything at all, apart from her role at the school. "Do you read *Rip Kirby*?"

"Do you read *Orphan Annie*?"

148

"Do you read *Betsy and the Boys*?"

"You haven't had hardly any Cracker Jack," I said. "Have some. Take a whole handful."

Myra looked into the box. "There's a prize in there," she said. She pulled it out. It was a brooch, a little tin butterfly, painted gold with bits of coloured glass stuck onto it to look like jewels. She held it in her brown hand, smiling slightly.

I said, "Do you like that?"

Myra said, "I like them blue stones. Blue stones are sapphires."

"I know. My birthstone is sapphire. What is your birthstone?"

"I don't know."

"When is your birthday?"

"July."

"Then yours is ruby."

"I like sapphire better," said Myra. "I like yours." She handed me the brooch.

"You keep it," I said. "Finders keepers."

Myra kept holding it out, as if she did not know what I meant. "Finders keepers," I said.

"It was your Cracker Jack," said Myra, scared and solemn. "You bought it."

"Well you found it."

"No—" said Myra.

"Go on!" I said. "Here, I'll *give* it to you." I took the brooch from her and pushed it back into her hand.

We were both surprised. We looked at each other; I flushed but Myra did not. I realized the pledge as our fingers touched; I was panicky, but *all right*. I thought, I can come early and walk with her other mornings. I can go and talk to her at recess. Why not? *Why not?*

Myra put the brooch in her pocket. She said, "I can wear it on my good dress. My good dress is blue."

149

I knew it would be. Myra wore out her good dresses at school. Even in midwinter among the plaid wool skirts and serge tunics, she glimmered sadly in sky-blue taffeta, in dusty turquoise crepe, a grown woman's dress made over, weighted by a big bow at the V of the neck and folding empty over Myra's narrow chest.

And I was glad she had not put it on. If someone asked her where she got it, and she told them, what would I say?

It was the day after this, or the week after, that Myra did not come to school. Often she was kept at home to help. But this time she did not come back. For a week, then two weeks, her desk was empty. Then we had a moving day at school, and Myra's books were taken out of her desk and put on a shelf in the closet. Miss Darling said, "We'll find a seat when she comes back." And she stopped calling Myra's name when she took attendance.

Jimmy Sayla did not come to school either, having no one to take him to the bathroom.

In the fourth week or the fifth, that Myra had been away, Gladys Healey came to school and said, "Do you know what— Myra Sayla is sick in the hospital."

It was true. Gladys Healey had an aunt who was a nurse. Gladys put up her hand in the middle of Spelling and told Miss Darling. "I thought you might like to know," she said. "Oh yes," said Miss Darling. "I do know."

"What has she got?" we said to Gladys.

And Gladys said, "Akemia, or something. And she has blood transfusions." She said to Miss Darling, "My aunt is a nurse."

So Miss Darling had the whole class write Myra a letter, in which everybody said, "Dear Myra, We are all writing you a letter. We hope you will soon be better and be back to school, Yours truly. . . ." And Miss Darling said, "I've thought of something. Who would like to go up to the hospital and visit Myra on the twentieth of March, for a birthday party?"

I said, "Her birthday's in July."

"I know," said Miss Darling. "It's the twentieth of July. So this year she could have it on the twentieth of March, because she's sick."

"But her *birthday* is in July."

"Because she's sick," said Miss Darling, with a warning shrillness. "The cook at the hospital would make a cake and you could all give a little present, twenty-five cents or so. It would have to be between two and four, because that's visiting hours. And we couldn't all go, it'd be too many. So who wants to go and who wants to stay here and do supplementary reading?"

We all put up our hands. Miss Darling got out the spelling records and picked out the first fifteen, twelve girls and three boys. Then the three boys did not want to go so she picked out the next three girls. And I do not know when it was, but I think it was probably at this moment that the birthday party of Myra Sayla became fashionable.

Perhaps it was because Gladys Healey had an aunt who was a nurse, perhaps it was the excitement of sickness and hospitals, or simply the fact that Myra was so entirely, impressively set free of all the rules and conditions of our lives. We began to talk of her as if she were something we owned, and her party became a cause; with womanly heaviness we discussed it at recess, and decided that twenty-five cents was too low.

We all went up to the hospital on a sunny afternoon when the snow was melting, carrying our presents, and a nurse led us upstairs, single file, and down a hall past half-closed doors and dim conversations. She and Miss Darling kept saying, "Sh-sh," but we were going on tiptoe anyway; our hospital demeanor was perfect.

At this small country hospital there was no children's ward, and Myra was not really a child; they had put her in with two grey old women. A nurse was putting screens around them as we came in.

Myra was sitting up in bed in a bulky stiff hospital gown. Her hair was down, the long braids falling over her shoulders and down the coverlet. But her face was the same, always the same.

She had been told something about the party, Miss Darling said, so the surprise would not upset her; but it seemed she had not believed, or had not understood what it was. She watched us as she used to watch in the school grounds when we played.

"Well, here we are!" said Miss Darling. "Here we are!"

And we said, "Happy birthday, Myra! Hello, Myra, happy birthday!" Myra said, "My birthday is in July." Her voice was lighter than ever, drifting, expressionless.

"Never mind when it is, really," said Miss Darling. "Pretend it's now! How old are you, Myra?"

"Eleven," Myra said. "In July."

Then we all took off our coats and emerged in our party dresses, and laid our presents, in their pale flowery wrappings, on Myra's bed. Some of our mothers had made immense, complicated bows of fine satin ribbon, some of them had even taped on little bouquets of imitation roses and lilies of the valley. "Here Myra," we said, "here Myra, happy birthday." Myra did not look at us, but at the ribbons, pink and blue and speckled with silver, and the miniature bouquets; they pleased her, as the butterfly had done. An innocent look came into her face, a partial, private smile.

"Open them, Myra," said Miss Darling. "They're for you!"

Myra gathered the presents around her, fingering them, with this smile, and a cautious realization, an unexpected pride. She said, "Saturday I'm going to London to St. Joseph's Hospital."

"That's where my mother was at," somebody said. "We went and saw her. They've got all nuns there."

"My father's sister is a nun," said Myra calmly.

She began to unwrap the presents, with an air that not even Gladys could have bettered, folding the tissue paper and the ribbons, and drawing out books and puzzles and cutouts as if they were all prizes she had won. Miss Darling said that maybe she should say thank you and the person's name with every gift she opened, to make sure she knew whom it was from, and so Myra said, "Thank you, Mary Louise, thank you, Carol," and when she came to mine she said, "Thank you, Helen." Everyone explained their presents to her and there was talking and excitement and a little gaiety, which Myra presided over, though she was not gay. A cake was brought in with *Happy Birthday Myra* written on it, pink on white, and eleven candles. Miss Darling lit the candles and we all sang "Happy Birthday to You," and cried, "Make a wish, Myra, make a wish—" and Myra blew them out. Then we all had cake and strawberry ice cream.

At four o'clock a buzzer sounded and the nurse took out what was left of the cake, and the dirty dishes, and we put on our coats to go home. Everybody said, "Goodbye, Myra," and Myra sat in the bed watching us go, her back straight, not supported by any pillow, her hands resting on the gifts. But at the door I heard her call; she called, "Helen!" Only a couple of the others heard; Miss Darling did not hear, she had gone out ahead. I went back to the bed.

Myra said, "I got too many things. You take something."

"What?" I said. "It's for your birthday. You always get a lot at a birthday."

"Well you take something," Myra said. She picked up a leatherette case with a mirror in it, a comb and a nail file and a natural lipstick and a small handkerchief edged with gold thread. I had noticed it before. "You take that," she said.

"Don't you want it?"

"You take it." She put it into my hand. Our fingers touched again.

"When I come back from London," Myra said, "you can come and play at my place after school."

"Okay," I said. Outside the hospital window there was a clear carrying sound of somebody playing in the street, maybe chasing with the last snowballs of the year. This sound made Myra, her triumph and her bounty, and most of all her future in which she had found this place for me, turn shadowy, turn dark. All the presents on the bed, the folded paper and ribbons, those guilt-tinged offerings, had passed into this shadow, they were no longer innocent objects to be touched, exchanged, accepted without danger. I didn't want to take the case now but I could not think how to get out of it, what lie to tell. I'll give it away, I thought, I won't ever play with it. I would let my little brother pull it apart.

The nurse came back, carrying a glass of chocolate milk.

"What's the matter, didn't you hear the buzzer?"

So I was released, set free by the barriers which now closed about Myra, her unknown, exalted, ether-smelling hospital

154

world, and by the treachery of my own heart. "Well thank you," I said. "Thank you for the thing. Goodbye."

Did Myra ever say goodbye? Not likely. She sat in her high bed, her delicate brown neck rising out of a hospital gown too big for her, her brown carved face immune to treachery, her offering perhaps already forgotten, prepared to be set apart for legendary uses, as she was even in the back porch at school.

THE WHITE CIRCLE

John Bell Clayton

As soon as I saw Anvil squatting up in the tree like some hateful creature that belonged in trees I knew I had to take a beating and I knew the kind of beating it would be. But still I had to let it be that way because this went beyond any matter of courage or shame.

The tree was *mine*. I want no doubt about that. It was a seedling that grew out of the slaty bank beside the dry creek-mark across the road from the house, and the thirteen small apples it had borne that year were the thirteen most beautiful things on this beautiful earth.

The day I was twelve Father took me up to the barn to look at the colts—Saturn, Jupiter, Devil, and Moonkissed, the whiteface. Father took a cigar out of his vest pocket and put one foot on the bottom plank of the fence and leaned both elbows on the top of the fence and his face looked quiet and pleased and proud and I liked the way he looked because it was as if he had a little joke or surprise that would turn out nice for me.

"Tucker," Father said presently, "I am not unaware of the momentousness of this day. Now there are four of the finest colts in Augusta County; if there are four any finer anywhere in Virginia I don't know where you'd find them unless Arthur Hancock over in Albemarle would have them." Father took one elbow off the fence and looked at me. "Now do you suppose," he asked, in that fine, free, good humor, "that if I were to offer you a little token to commemorate this occasion you could make a choice?"

"Yes sir," I said.

"Which one?" Father asked. "Devil? He's wild."

"No sir," I said. "I would like to have the apple tree below the gate."

Father looked at me for at least a minute. You would have to understand his pride in his colts to understand the way he looked. But at twelve how could I express how *I* felt? My setting such store in having the tree as my own had something to do with the coloring of the apples as they hung among the green leaves; it had something also to do with their ripening, not in autumn when the world was full of apples, but in midsummer when you *wanted* them; but it had more to do with a way of life that had come down through the generations. I would have given one of the apples to Janie. I would have made of it a ceremony. While I would not have said the words, because at twelve you have no such words, I would have handed over the apple with something like this in mind: "Janie, I want to give you this apple. It came from my tree. The tree stands on my father's land. Before my father had the land it belonged to his father, and before that it belonged to my great-grandfather. It's the English family land. It's almost sacred. My possession of this tree forges of me a link in this owning ancestry that must go back clear beyond Moses and all the old Bible folks."

Father looked at me for that slow, peculiar minute in our lives. "All right, son," he said. "The tree is yours in fee simple to bargain, sell, and convey, or to keep and nurture and eventually hand down to your heirs or assigns forever unto eternity. You have a touch of poetry in your soul and that fierce, proud love of the land in your heart; when you grow up I hope you don't drink too much."

I didn't know what he meant by that but the tree was mine and now there perched Anvil, callously munching one of my thirteen apples and stowing the rest inside his ragged shirt until it bulged out in ugly lumps. I knew the apples pressed cold against his hateful belly and to me the coldness was a sickening evil.

I picked a rock up out of the dust of the road and tore across the creek bed and said, "All right, Anvil—climb down!"

Anvil's milky eyes batted at me under the strangely fair eyebrows. There was not much expression on his face. "Yaannh!" he said. "You stuck-up little priss, you hit me with that rock. You just do!"

"Anvil," I said again, "climb down. They're my apples."

Anvil quit munching for a minute and grinned at me. "You want an apple? I'll give you one. Yaannh!" He suddenly cocked back his right arm and cracked me on the temple with the half-eaten apple.

I let go with the rock and it hit a limb with a dull chub sound and Anvil said, "You're fixin' to git it—you're real-ly fixin' to git it."

"I'll shake you down," I said. "I'll shake you clear down."

"Clear down?" Anvil chortled. "Where do you think I'm at? Up on top of Walker Mountain? It wouldn't hurt none if I was to fall out of this runty bush on my head."

I grabbed one of his bare feet and pulled backwards, and down Anvil came amidst a flutter of broken twigs and leaves.

159

We both hit the ground. I hopped up and Anvil arose with a faintly vexed expression.

He hooked a leg in back of my knees and shoved a paw against my chin. I went down in the slate. He got down and pinioned my arms with his knees. I tried to kick him in the back of the head but could only flail my feet helplessly in the air.

"You might as well quit kickin'," he said.

He took one of my apples from his shirt and began eating it, almost absent-mindedly.

"You dirty filthy stinkin' sow," I said.

He snorted. "I couldn't be a sow, but you take that back."

"I wish you were fryin' in the middle of hell right this minute."

"Take back the stinkin' part," Anvil said thoughtfully. "I don't stink."

He pressed his knees down harder, pinching and squeezing the flesh of my arms.

I sobbed, "I take back the stinkin' part."

"That's better," Anvil said.

He ran a finger back into his jaw to dislodge a fragment of apple from his teeth. For a moment he examined the fragment and then wiped it on my cheek.

"I'm goin' to tell Father," I said desperately.

"'Father,'" Anvil said with falsetto mimicry. "'Father.' Say 'Old Man.' You think your old man is some stuff on a stick, don't you? You think he don't walk on the ground, don't you? You think you and your whole stuck-up family don't walk on the ground. Say 'Old Man.'"

"Go to hell!"

"Shut up your blubberin'. Say 'Old Man.'"

"Old Man. I wish you were dead."

160

"Yaannh!" Anvil said. "Stop blubberin'. Now call me 'Uncle Anvil.' Say 'Uncle Sweetie Peetie Tweetie Beg-Your-Pardon Uncle Anvil.' Say it!"

"Uncle Sweetie . . . Uncle Peetie, Tweetie Son-of-a-Bitch Anvil."

He caught my hair in his hands and wallowed my head against the ground until I said every bitter word of it. Three times.

Anvil tossed away a spent, maltreated core that had been my apple. He gave my head one final thump upon the ground and said "Yaannh!" again in a satisfied way.

He released me and got up. I lay there with my face muscles twitching in outrage.

Anvil looked down at me. "Stop blubberin'," he commanded.

"I'm not cryin'," I said.

I was lying there with a towering, homicidal detestation, planning to kill Anvil—and the thought of it had a sweetness like summer fruit.

There were times when I had no desire to kill Anvil. I remember the day his father showed up at the school. He was a dirty, half-crazy, itinerant knickknack peddler. He had a club and he told the principal he was going to beat the meanness out of Anvil or beat him to death. Anvil scudded under a desk and lay there trembling and whimpering until the principal finally drove the ragged old man away. I had no hatred for Anvil then.

But another day, just for the sheer filthy meanness of it, he crawled through a classroom window after school hours and befouled the floor. And the number of times he pushed over smaller boys, just to see them hit the packed hard earth of the schoolyard and to watch the fright on their faces as they ran away, was more than I could count.

And still another day he walked up to me as I leaned against the warmth of the schoolhack shed in the sunlight, feeling the nice warmth of the weather-beaten boards.

"They hate me," he said dismally. "They hate me because my old man's crazy."

As I looked at Anvil I felt that in the background I was seeing that demented, bitter father trudging his lonely, vicious way through the world.

"They don't hate you," I lied. "Anyway I don't hate you." That was true. At that moment I didn't hate him. "How about comin' home and stayin' all night with me?"

So after school Anvil went along with me—and threw rocks at me all the way home.

Now I had for him no soft feeling of any kind. I planned—practically—his extinction as he stood there before me commanding me to cease the blubbering out of my heart.

"Shut up now," Anvil said. "I never hurt you. Stop blubberin'."

"I'm not cryin'," I said.

"You're still mad though." He looked at me appraisingly.

"No, I'm not," I lied. "I'm not even mad. I was a little bit mad, but not now."

"Well, whattaya look so funny around the mouth and eyes for?"

"I don't know. Let's go up to the barn and play."

"Play whut?" Anvil looked at me truculently. He didn't know whether to be suspicious or flattered. "I'm gettin' too big to play. To play much, anyway," he added undecidedly. "I might play a little bit if it ain't some sissy game."

"We'll play anything," I said eagerly.

"All right," he said. "Race you to the barn. You start."

I started running toward the wire fence and at the third step he stuck his foot between my legs and I fell forward on my face.

"Yaannh!" he croaked. "That'll learn you."

"Learn me what?" I asked as I got up. "Learn me what?" It seemed important to know that. Maybe it would make some difference in what I planned to do to Anvil. It seemed very important to know what it was that Anvil wanted to, and never could, teach me and the world.

"It'll just learn you," he said doggedly. "Go ahead, I won't trip you anymore."

So we climbed the wire fence and raced across the burned field the hogs ranged in.

We squeezed through the heavy sliding doors onto the barn floor, and the first thing that caught Anvil's eye was the irregular circle that Father had painted there. He wanted to know what it was and I said "Nothing" because I wasn't yet quite ready, and Anvil forgot about it for the moment and wanted to play jumping from the barn floor out to the top of the fresh rick of golden straw.

I said, "No. Who wants to do that, anyway?"

"I do," said Anvil. "Jump, you puke. Go ahead and jump!"

I didn't want to jump. The barn had been built on a hill. In front the ground came up level with the barn floor, but in back the floor was even with the top of the straw rick with four wide, terrible, yawning feet between.

I said, "Nawh, there's nothin' to jumpin'."

"Oh, there ain't, hanh!" said Anvil. "Well, try it—"

He gave me a shove and I went out into terrifying space. He leaped after and upon me and we hit the pillowy side of the straw rick and tumbled to the ground in a smothering slide.

"That's no fun," I said, getting up and brushing the chaff from my face and hair.

Anvil himself had lost interest in it by now and was idly munching another of my apples.

"I know somethin'," I said. "I know a good game. Come on, I'll show you."

Anvil stung me on the leg with the apple as I raced through the door of the cutting room. When we reached the barn floor his eyes again fell on the peculiar white circle. "That's to play prisoner's base with," I said. "That's the base."

"That's a funny-lookin' base," he said suspiciously. "I never saw any base that looked like that."

I could feel my muscles tensing, but I wasn't particularly excited. I didn't trust myself to look up toward the roof where the big mechanical hayfork hung suspended from the long metal track that ran back over the steaming mows of alfalfa and red clover. The fork had vicious sharp prongs that had never descended to the floor except on one occasion Anvil knew nothing about.

I think Father had been drinking the day he bought the hayfork in Staunton. It was an unwieldy, involved contraption of ropes, triggers, and pulleys which took four men to operate. A man came out to install the fork, and for several days he climbed up and down ladders, bolting the track in place and arranging the various gadgets. Finally, when he said it was ready, Father had a load of hay pulled into the barn and called the men in from the fields to watch and assist in the demonstration.

I don't remember the details. I just remember that something went very badly wrong. The fork suddenly plunged down with a peculiar ripping noise and embedded itself in the back of one of the workhorses. Father said very little. He simply painted the big white circle on the barn floor, had the fork hauled back up to the top, and fastened the trigger around the rung of a stationary ladder eight feet off the floor, where no one could inadvertently pull it.

Then he said quietly, "I don't ever want anyone ever to touch this trip rope or to have occasion to step inside this circle."

So that was why I didn't now look up toward the fork.

"I don't want to play no sissy prisoner's base," Anvil said. "Let's find a nest of young pigeons."

"All right," I lied. "I know where there's a nest. But one game of prisoner's base first."

"You don't know where there's any pigeon nest," Anvil said. "You wouldn't have the nerve to throw them up against the barn if you did."

"Yes, I would too," I protested. "Now let's play one game of prisoner's base. Get in the circle and shut your eyes and start countin'."

"Oh, all right," Anvil agreed wearily. "Let's get it over with and find the pigeons. Ten, ten, double ten, forty-five—"

"Right in the middle of the circle," I told him. "And count slow. How'm I goin' to hide if you count that way?"

Anvil now counted more slowly. "Five, ten, fifteen—"

I gave Anvil one last vindictive look and sprang up the stationary ladder and swung out on the trip rope of the unpredictable hayfork with all my puny might.

The fork's whizzing descent was accompanied by that peculiar ripping noise. Anvil must have jumped instinctively. The fork missed him by several feet.

For a moment Anvil stood absolutely still. He turned around and saw the fork, still shimmering from its impact with the floor. His face became exactly the pale green of the carbide we burned in our acetylene lighting plant at the house. Then he looked at me, at the expression on my face, and his Adam's apple bobbed queerly up and down, and a little stream of water trickled down his right trouser leg and over his bare foot.

"You tried to kill me," he said thickly.

He did not come toward me. Instead, he sat down. He shook his head sickly. After a few sullen, bewildered moments he reached into his shirt and began hauling out my apples one by one.

"You can have your stinkin' old apples," he said. "You'd do that for a few dried-up little apples. Your old man owns everything in sight. I ain't got nothin'. Go ahead and keep your stinkin' old apples."

He got to his feet and slowly walked out of the door.

Since swinging off the trip rope I had neither moved nor spoken. For a moment more I stood motionless and voiceless and then I ran over and grabbed up the nine apples that were left and called, "Anvil! Anvil!" He continued across the field without even pausing.

I yelled, "Anvil! Wait, I'll give them to you."

Anvil climbed the fence without looking back and set off down the road toward the store. Every few steps he kicked his wet trouser leg.

Three sparrows flew out of the door in a dusty, chattering spiral. Then there was only the image of the hayfork shimmering and terrible in the great and growing and accusing silence and emptiness of the barn.

READING NONFICTION

Some nonfiction texts, like autobiographies or accounts of historical events, can read like stories. Others, like instruction manuals and some textbooks, are written purely to give information. In the Great Books Roundtable program, you will be reading nonfiction texts that include both narrative (story) and informational parts and that also raise questions for discussion.

Below are some questions you can ask yourself to help you better understand a nonfiction selection and discover issues you want to discuss. Try asking yourself these questions after your first reading of the text. Then, after rereading, consider how your answers have changed.

The reading strategies on pages xxii–xxiii are also helpful when reading nonfiction.

SUGGESTED QUESTIONS FOR NONFICTION

- How would you describe the author's tone?
- To whom does the author seem to be speaking?
- What is the author's attitude toward his or her subject?
- What is the structure of the text—is it like a list, a story, a persuasive essay, or something else? What is the effect of putting it together this way?
- What is the author trying to make you think, feel, or believe?
- Is the author asking you to take some kind of action?

WOLF

Loren Eiseley

As to what happened next, it is possible to maintain
that the hand of heaven was involved, and also possible
to say that when men are desperate no one can stand
up to them.

—Xenophon

A time comes when creatures whose destinies have crossed
somewhere in the remote past are forced to appraise each other
as though they were total strangers. I had been huddled beside
the fire one winter night, with the wind prowling outside and
shaking the windows. The big shepherd dog on the hearth
before me occasionally glanced up affectionately, sighed, and
slept. I was working, actually, amidst the debris of a far greater
winter. On my desk lay the lance points of ice-age hunters
and the heavy leg bone of a fossil bison. No remnants of flesh
attached to these relics. The deed lay more than ten thousand
years remote. It was represented here by naked flint and by
bone so mineralized it rang when struck. As I worked on in my
little circle of light, I absently laid the bone beside me on the

171

floor. The hour had crept toward midnight. A grating noise, a heavy rasping of big teeth diverted me. I looked down.

The dog had risen. That rock-hard fragment of a vanished beast was in his jaws and he was mouthing it with a fierce intensity I had never seen exhibited by him before.

"Wolf," I exclaimed, and stretched out my hand. The dog backed up but did not yield. A low and steady rumbling began to rise in his chest, something out of a long-gone midnight. There was nothing in that bone to taste, but ancient shapes were moving in his mind and determining his utterance. Only fools gave up bones. He was warning me.

"Wolf," I chided again.

As I advanced, his teeth showed and his mouth wrinkled to strike. The rumbling rose to a direct snarl. His flat head swayed low and wickedly as a reptile's above the floor. I was the most loved object in his universe, but the past was fully alive in him now. Its shadows were whispering in his mind. I knew he was not bluffing. If I made another step he would strike.

Yet his eyes were strained and desperate. "Do not," something pleaded in the back of them, some affectionate thing that had followed at my heel all the days of his mortal life, "do not force me. I am what I am and cannot be otherwise because of the shadows. Do not reach out. You are a man, and my very god. I love you, but do not put out your hand. It is midnight. We are in another time, in the snow."

"The *other* time," the steady rumbling continued while I paused, "the other time in the snow, the big, the final, the terrible snow, when the shape of this thing I hold spelled life. I will not give it up. I cannot. The shadows will not permit me. Do not put out your hand."

I stood silent, looking into his eyes, and heard his whisper through. Slowly I drew back in understanding. The snarl diminished, ceased. As I retreated, the bone slumped to the floor. He placed a paw upon it, warningly.

And were there no shadows in my own mind, I wondered. Had I not for a moment, in the grip of that savage utterance, been about to respond, to hurl myself upon him over an invisible haunch ten thousand years removed? Even to me the shadows had whispered—to me, the scholar in his study.

"Wolf," I said, but this time, holding a familiar leash, I spoke from the door indifferently. "A walk in the snow." Instantly from his eyes that other visitant receded. The bone was left lying. He came eagerly to my side, accepting the leash and taking it in his mouth as always.

A blizzard was raging when we went out, but he paid no heed. On his thick fur the driving snow was soon clinging heavily. He frolicked a little—though usually he was a grave dog—making up to me for something still receding in his mind. I felt the snowflakes fall upon my face, and stood thinking of another time, and another time still, until I was moving from midnight to midnight under ever more remote and vaster snows. Wolf came to my side with a little whimper. It was he who was civilized now. "Come back to the fire," he nudged gently, "or you will be lost." Automatically I took the leash he offered. He led me safely home and into the house.

"We have been very far away," I told him solemnly. "I think there is something in us that we had both better try to forget." Sprawled on the rug, Wolf made no response except to thump his tail feebly out of courtesy. Already he was mostly asleep and dreaming. By the movement of his feet I could see he was running far upon some errand in which I played no part.

Softly I picked up his bone—our bone, rather—and replaced it high on a shelf in my cabinet. As I snapped off the light the white glow from the window seemed to augment itself and shine with a deep, glacial blue. As far as I could see, nothing moved in the long aisles of my neighbor's woods. There was no visible track, and certainly no sound from the living. The snow continued to fall steadily, but the wind, and the shadows it had brought, had vanished.

COLTER'S WAY

Sebastian Junger

Late in the summer of 1808 two fur trappers named John Colter and John Potts decided to paddle up the Missouri River, deep into Blackfeet territory, to look for beaver. Colter had been there twice before; still, they couldn't have picked a more dangerous place. The area, now known as Montana, was blank wilderness, and the Blackfeet had been implacably hostile to white men ever since their first contact with Lewis and Clark several years earlier. Colter and Potts were working for a fur trader named Manuel Lisa, who had built a fort at the confluence of the Yellowstone and Bighorn rivers. One morning in mid-August they loaded up their canoes, shoved off into the Yellowstone, and started paddling north.

Colter was the better known of the two men. Tall, lean, and a wicked shot, he had spent more time in the wilderness than probably any white man alive—first as a hunter on the Lewis and Clark expedition, then two more years guiding and trapping along the Yellowstone. The previous winter he'd set out alone, with nothing but a rifle, a buffalo-skin blanket, and a thirty-pound pack, to complete a several-month trek through what is now Montana, Idaho, and Wyoming. He saw steam geysers in an area near present-day Cody, Wyoming, that was later dubbed Colter's Hell by disbelievers. Within weeks of arriving back at Lisa's fort in the spring of 1808, he headed right back out again, this time up to the Three Forks area of Montana, where he'd been with Lewis and Clark almost three years earlier. His trip was cut short when he was shot in the leg during a fight with some Blackfeet, and he returned to Lisa's fort to let the wound heal. No sooner was he better, though, than he went straight back to Three Forks, this time with John Potts. The two men quickly amassed almost a ton of pelts, but every day they spent in Blackfeet territory was pushing their luck. Finally, sometime in the fall, their luck ran out.

As they paddled the Jefferson River, five hundred Blackfeet Indians suddenly swarmed toward them along the bank. Potts grabbed his rifle and killed one of them with a single shot, but he may have done that just to spare himself a slow death; the Blackfeet immediately shot him so full of arrows that "he was made a riddle of," as Colter put it. Colter surrendered and was stripped naked. One of the Blackfeet asked whether he was a good runner. Colter had the presence of mind to say no, so the Blackfeet told him he could run for his life; when they caught him, they would kill him. Naked, unarmed, and given a head start of only a couple of hundred yards, Colter started to run.

He was, as it turned out, a good runner—very good. He headed for the Madison River, six miles away, and by the time he was halfway there, he'd already outdistanced every Blackfoot except one. His pursuer was carrying a spear, and Colter spun around unexpectedly, wrestled it away from him, and killed him with it. He kept running until he got to the river, dived in, and hid inside a logjam until the Blackfeet got tired of looking for him. He emerged after nightfall, swam several miles down-stream, then clambered out and started walking. Lisa's fort was nearly two hundred miles away. He arrived a week and a half later, his feet in shreds.

Clearly, Colter was a man who sought risk. After two brutal years with Lewis and Clark, all it took was a chance encounter with a couple of itinerant trappers for Colter to turn around and head back into Indian territory. And the following summer—after three straight years in the wild—Manuel Lisa convinced him to do the same thing. Even Colter's narrow escape didn't scare him off; soon after recovering from his ordeal, he returned to the Three Forks area to retrieve his traps and had to flee from the Blackfeet once again. And in April 1810 he survived another Blackfeet attack on a new stockade at Three Forks, an attack that left five men dead. Finally Colter had had enough. He traveled down the Missouri and reached St. Louis by the end of May. He married a young woman and settled on a farm near Dundee, Missouri. Where the Blackfeet had failed, civilization succeeded: he died just two years later.

Given the trajectory of Colter's life, one could say that the wilderness was good for him, kept him alive. It was there that he functioned at the outer limits of his abilities, a state that humans have always thrived on. "Dangers . . . seemed to have for him a kind of fascination," another fur trapper who knew Colter said. It must have been while under the effect of that fascination that Colter felt most alive, most potent. That was why he stayed in the wilderness for six straight years; that was why he kept sneaking up to Three Forks to test his skills against the Blackfeet.

Fifty years later, whalers in New Bedford, Massachusetts, would find themselves unable to face life back home and—as miserable as they were—would sign up for another three years at sea. A hundred years after that, American soldiers at the end of their tours in Vietnam would realize they could not go back to civilian life and would volunteer for one more stint in hell.

"Their shirts and breeches of buckskin or elkskin had many patches sewed on with sinews, were worn thin between patches, were black from many campfires, and greasy from many meals," writes historian Bernard De Voto about the early trappers. "They were threadbare and filthy, they smelled bad, and any Mandan had lighter skin. They gulped rather than ate the tripes of buffalo. They had forgotten the use of chairs. Words and phrases, mostly obscene, of Nez Percé, Clatsop, Mandan, Chinook came naturally to their tongues."

None of these men had become trappers against his will; to one degree or another, they'd all volunteered for the job. However rough it was, it must have looked better than the alternative, which was—in one form or another—an uneventful life passed in society's embrace. For people like Colter, the one thing more terrifying than having something bad happen must have been to have nothing happen at all.

Modern society, of course, has perfected the art of having nothing happen at all. There is nothing particularly wrong with this except that for vast numbers of Americans, as life has become staggeringly easy, it has also become vaguely unfulfilling. Life in modern society is designed to eliminate as many unforeseen events as possible, and as inviting as that seems, it leaves us hopelessly underutilized. And that is where the idea of "adventure" comes in. The word comes from the Latin *adventura*, meaning "what must happen." An adventure is a situation where the outcome is not entirely within your control. It's up to fate, in other words. It should be pointed out that people whose lives are inherently dangerous, like coal miners or steelworkers, rarely seek "adventure." Like most things, danger ceases to be interesting as soon as you have no choice in the matter. For the rest of us, threats to our safety and comfort have been so completely wiped out that we have to go out of our way to create them.

About ten years ago a young rock climber named Dan Osman started free-soloing—climbing without a safety rope—on cliffs that had stymied some of the best climbers in the country. Falling was not an option. At about the same time, though, he began falling on purpose, jumping off cliffs tethered not by a bungee cord but by regular climbing rope. He found that if he calculated the arc of his fall just right, he could jump hundreds of feet and survive. Osman's father, a policeman, told a journalist named Andrew Todhunter, "Doing the work that I do, I have faced death many, many, many times. When it's over, you celebrate the fact that you're alive, you celebrate the fact that you have a family, you celebrate the fact that you can breathe. Everything, for a few instants, seems sweeter, brighter, louder. And I think this young man has reached a point where his awareness of life and living is far beyond what I could ever achieve."

Todhunter wrote a book about Osman called *Fall of the Phantom Lord*. A few months after the book came out, Osman died on a twelve-hundred-foot fall in Yosemite National Park. He had rigged up a rope that would allow him to jump off Leaning Tower, but after more than a dozen successful jumps by Osman and others, the rope snapped and Osman plummeted to the ground.

Colter of course would have thought Osman was crazy—risk your life for no good reason at all?—but he certainly would have understood the allure. Every time Colter went up to Three Forks, he was in effect free-soloing. Whether he survived or not was entirely up to him. No one was going to save him;

no one was going to come to his aid. It's the oldest game in the world—and perhaps the most compelling.

The one drawback to modern adventuring, however, is that people can mistake it for something it's not. The fact that someone can free-solo a sheer rock face or balloon halfway around the world is immensely impressive, but it's not strictly necessary. And because it's not necessary, it's not heroic. Society would continue to function quite well if no one ever climbed another mountain, but it would come grinding to a halt if roughnecks stopped working on oil rigs. Oddly, though, it's the mountaineers who are heaped with glory, not the roughnecks, who have a hard time even getting a date in an oil town. A roughneck who gets crushed tripping pipe or a firefighter who dies in a burning building has, in some ways, died a heroic death. But Dan Osman did not; he died because he voluntarily gambled with his life and lost. That makes him brave—unspeakably brave—but nothing more. Was his life worth the last jump? Undoubtedly not. Was his life worth living without those jumps? Apparently not. The task of every person alive is to pick a course between those two extremes.

I have only once been in a situation where everything depended on me—my own version of Colter's run. It's a ludicrous comparison except that for the age that I was, the stakes seemed every bit as high. When I was eleven, I went skiing for a week with a group of boys my age, and late one afternoon when we had nothing to do, we walked off into the pine forests around the resort. The snow was very deep, up to our waists in places, and we wallowed through slowly, taking turns breaking trail. After about half an hour, and deep into the woods now, we crested a hill and saw a small road down below us. We waited a few minutes, and sure enough, a car went by. We all threw snowballs at it. A few minutes later another one went by, and we let loose another volley.

Our snowballs weren't hitting their mark, so we worked our way down closer to the road and put together some really dense, heavy iceballs—ones that would throw like a baseball and hit just as hard. Then we waited, the woods getting darker and darker, and finally in the distance we heard the heavy whine of an eighteen-wheeler downshifting on a hill. A minute later it barreled around the turn, and at the last moment we all heaved our iceballs. Five or six big white splats blossomed on the windshield. That was followed by the ghastly yelp of an air brake.

It was a dangerous thing to do, of course: the driver was taking an icy road very fast, and the explosion of snow against his windshield must have made him jump right out of his skin. We didn't think of that, though; we just watched in puzzlement as the truck bucked to a stop. And then the driver's side door flew open and a man jumped out. And everyone started to run.

I don't know why he picked me, but he did. My friends scattered into the forest, no one saying a word, and when I looked back, the man was after me. He was so angry that strange grunts were coming out of him. I had never seen an adult that enraged. I ran harder and harder, but to my amazement, he just kept coming. We were all alone in the forest now, way out of earshot of my friends; it was just a race between him and me. I knew I couldn't afford to lose it; the man was too crazy, too determined, and there was no one around to intervene. I was on my own. *Adventura*—what must happen will happen.

Before I knew it, the man had drawn to within a few steps of me. Neither of us said a word; we just wallowed on through the snow, each engaged in our private agonies. It was a slow-motion race with unimaginable consequences. We struggled on for what seemed like miles but in reality was probably only a few hundred yards; the deep snow made it seem farther. In the end I outlasted him. He was a strong man, but he spent his days behind the wheel of a truck—smoking, no doubt—and he was no match for a terrified kid. With a groan of disgust he finally stopped and doubled over, swearing at me between breaths.

I kept running. I ran until his shouts had died out behind me and I couldn't stand up anymore, and then I collapsed in the snow. It was completely dark and the only sounds were the heaving of the wind through the trees and the liquid slamming of my heart. I lay there until I was calm, and then I got up and slowly made my way back to the resort. It felt as if I'd been someplace very far away and had come back to a world of tremendous frivolity and innocence. It was all lit up, peals of laughter coming from the bar, adults hobbling back and forth in ski boots and brightly colored parkas. "I've just come back from some other place," I thought. "I've just come back from some other place these people don't even know exists."

READING POETRY

If you are puzzled about what to make of a poem, you are not alone. Poems are meant to be read over and over and discovered slowly. Asking questions about a poem can help you uncover more of its meaning and think about it in new ways.

Below are some questions you can ask yourself to help you better understand a poem and discover issues you want to discuss. Try asking yourself these questions after you read the poem once or twice. Then, after a couple more readings, consider how your answers have changed.

SUGGESTED QUESTIONS FOR POETRY

About the Poem and the Audience

- Who is the poem's speaker?
- What situation or event is happening?
- Who or what is the audience?
- How does the title relate to the rest of the poem?
- Does the poem have to do with a particular moment in history?
- Does the poem have to do with a particular culture or society?

About Poetic Language and Form

- What kind of form does the poem have? How does it look on the page?

- Does the poem use words in an unusual way?

- Is the way the words sound (not just what they mean) an important element of the poem?

- Does the poem use images to make the reader feel a certain way?

- What is the tone? How do you know?

WAYS TO READ POETRY

Below are some ways to read and mark a poem that can help you further explore the author's choice of rhythm, language, and structure.

Recognize Rhythm

- With a partner, take turns reading the poem aloud several times. Experiment with each reading by exaggerating the syllables of words, speeding up or slowing down your reading, or clapping out the poem's rhythm while you read.

- Read the poem as a whole class, clapping, stomping, or walking in time to the poem's rhythm as you read.

Listen to Language

- With a partner, take turns reading the poem aloud several times. Experiment with each reading by exaggerating your mouth movements, stressing the consonants or vowels of certain words, or communicating with your voice how certain words make you feel.

- Underline some of the poem's repeated sounds or letters. Reread the poem aloud, stressing the repetitions you underlined.

See the Structure

- Trace the end of each line of the poem with a pencil (as if connecting dots) to see what pattern the poem makes on the page.
- Read the poem aloud, taking a breath or pausing at the end of each *sentence* in the poem—wherever there is a period, question mark, or exclamation point. Then read the poem again, taking a breath or pausing at each *line break*—wherever the author stops a line. Compare the two readings. How were they different? How did each one make you feel about the poem? Did you notice anything new in either reading?

HARLEM [2]

Langston Hughes

What happens to a dream deferred?

    Does it dry up
    like a raisin in the sun?
    Or fester like a sore—
    And then run?
    Does it stink like rotten meat?
    Or crust and sugar over—
    like a syrupy sweet?

    Maybe it just sags
    like a heavy load.

    Or does it explode?

AN IRISH AIRMAN FORESEES HIS DEATH

William Butler Yeats

I know that I shall meet my fate
Somewhere among the clouds above;
Those that I fight I do not hate,
Those that I guard I do not love;
My country is Kiltartan Cross,
My countrymen Kiltartan's poor,
No likely end could bring them loss
Or leave them happier than before.
Nor law, nor duty bade me fight,
Nor public men, nor cheering crowds,
A lonely impulse of delight
Drove to this tumult in the clouds;
I balanced all, brought all to mind,
The years to come seemed waste of breath,
A waste of breath the years behind
In balance with this life, this death.

[n]

E. E. Cummings

n
OthI
n

g can

s
urPas
s

the m

y
SteR
y

of

s
tilLnes
s

THE FORT

Marie Howe

It was a kind of igloo
made from branches and weeds, a dome
with an aboveground tunnel entrance
the boys crawled through on their knees,
and a campfire in the center
because smoke came out of a hole in the roof,
and we couldn't go there. I
don't even remember trying, not
inside. Although I remember
a deal we didn't keep—so many
Dr Peppers which nobody drank,
and my brother standing outside it
like a chief: bare-chested, weary
from labor, proud, dignified,
and talking to us as if we could never
understand a thing he said because
he had made this thing and we had not,
and could not have done it, not
in a thousand years—true knowledge
and disdain when he looked at us.
For those weeks the boys didn't chase us.
They busied themselves with patching
the fort and sweeping the dirt outside
the entrance, a village of boys

who had a house to clean, women
in magazines, cigarettes and soda and
the strange self-contained voices they used
to speak to each other with.
And we approached the clearing where
their fort was like deer in winter
hungry for any small thing—what
they had made without us.
We wanted to watch them live there.

BICYCLES

Andrei Voznesensky

For V. Bokov

The bicycles lie
In the woods, in the dew.
    Between the birch trees
    The highroad gleams.

They fell, fell down
Mudguard to mudguard,
    Handlebar to handlebar
    Pedal to pedal.

And you can't
Wake them up!
    Petrified monsters,
    Their chains entwined.

Huge and surprised
They stare at the sky.
    Above them, green dusk
    Resin, and bumblebees.

In the luxurious
Rustling of camomile, peppermint
    Leaves they lie. Forgotten,
    Asleep. Asleep.

SNAKE

D. H. Lawrence

A snake came to my water-trough
On a hot, hot day, and I in pyjamas for the heat,
To drink there.

In the deep, strange-scented shade of the great dark carob tree
I came down the steps with my pitcher
And must wait, must stand and wait, for there he was at the
    trough before me.

He reached down from a fissure in the earth-wall in the gloom
And trailed his yellow-brown slackness soft-bellied down, over
    the edge of the stone trough
And rested his throat upon the stone bottom,
And where the water had dripped from the tap, in a small
    clearness,
He sipped with his straight mouth,
Softly drank through his straight gums, into his slack
    long body,
Silently.

Someone was before me at my water-trough,
And I, like a second-comer, waiting.

He lifted his head from his drinking, as cattle do,
And looked at me vaguely, as drinking cattle do,
And flickered his two-forked tongue from his lips, and mused a
    moment,
And stooped and drank a little more,
Being earth-brown, earth-golden from the burning bowels of the
    earth
On the day of Sicilian July, with Etna smoking.

The voice of my education said to me
He must be killed,
For in Sicily the black, black snakes are innocent, the gold are
    venomous.

And voices in me said, If you were a man
You would take a stick and break him now, and finish him off.

But must I confess how I liked him,
How glad I was he had come like a guest in quiet, to drink at
    my water-trough
And depart peaceful, pacified, and thankless,
Into the burning bowels of this earth?

Was it cowardice, that I dared not kill him?
Was it perversity, that I longed to talk to him?
Was it humility, to feel so honoured?
I felt so honoured.

And yet those voices:
If you were not afraid, you would kill him!

And truly I was afraid, I was most afraid,
But even so, honoured still more
That he should seek my hospitality
From out the dark door of the secret earth.

He drank enough
And lifted his head, dreamily, as one who has drunken,
And flickered his tongue like a forked night on the air, so black,
Seeming to lick his lips,
And looked around like a god, unseeing, into the air,
And slowly turned his head,
And slowly, very slowly, as if thrice adream
Proceeded to draw his slow length curving round
And climb again the broken bank of my wall-face.

And as he put his head into that dreadful hole,
And as he slowly drew up, snake-easing his shoulders, and
    entered farther,
A sort of horror, a sort of protest against his withdrawing into that
    horrid black hole,
Deliberately going into the blackness, and slowly drawing himself
    after,
Overcame me now his back was turned.

I looked round, I put down my pitcher,
I picked up a clumsy log
And threw it at the water-trough with a clatter.

I think it did not hit him,
But suddenly that part of him that was left behind convulsed
    in an undignified haste,
Writhed like lightning, and was gone
Into the black hole, the earth-lipped fissure in the wall-front,
At which, in the intense still noon, I stared with fascination.

And immediately I regretted it.
I thought how paltry, how vulgar, what a mean act!
I despised myself and the voices of my accursed human education.

And I thought of the albatross,
And I wished he would come back, my snake.

For he seemed to me again like a king,
Like a king in exile, uncrowned in the underworld,
Now due to be crowned again.

And so, I missed my chance with one of the lords
Of life.
And I have something to expiate:
A pettiness.

ACKNOWLEDGMENTS

The White Umbrella, by Gish Jen, first published in THE YALE REVIEW: 1984. Copyright © 1984 by Gish Jen. Reprinted by permission of the Melanie Jackson Agency, LLC.

Harrison Bergeron, from WELCOME TO THE MONKEY HOUSE, by Kurt Vonnegut Jr. Copyright © 1961 by Kurt Vonnegut Jr. Reprinted by permission of Dell Publishing, a division of Random House, Inc.

The First Day, from LOST IN THE CITY: STORIES BY EDWARD P. JONES, by Edward P. Jones. Copyright © 1992, 2005 by Edward P. Jones. Reprinted by permission of HarperCollins Publishers.

Props for Faith, extract from FLOATING IN MY MOTHER'S PALM: A NOVEL, by Ursula Hegi. Copyright © 1990 by Ursula Hegi. Reprinted by permission of Simon and Schuster, Inc.

El Diablo de La Cienega, from DANGEROUS MEN, by Geoffrey Becker. Copyright © 1995 by Geoffrey Becker. Reprinted by permission of the University of Pittsburgh Press.

The Cat and the Coffee Drinkers, from WHERE SHE BRUSHED HER HAIR AND OTHER STORIES, by Max Steele. Copyright © 1963, 1969 by Max Steele. Reprinted by permission of the Literary Estate of Maxwell Steele.

The Box House and the Snow, from COME TOGETHER, FALL APART, by Cristina Henríquez. Copyright © 2006 by Cristina Henríquez. Reprinted by permission of Riverhead Books, an imprint of Penguin Group (USA) Inc.

I Just Kept On Smiling, from FLORAL STREET, by Simon Burt. Copyright © 1983, 1986 by Simon Burt. Reprinted by permission of the author.

Mercedes Kane, from HERE'S YOUR HAT WHAT'S YOUR HURRY: STORIES BY ELIZABETH McCRACKEN, by Elizabeth McCracken. Copyright © 1993 by Elizabeth McCracken. Reprinted by permission of Dunow, Carlson and Lerner Literary Agency.

Sandra Street, from CRICKET IN THE ROAD, by Michael Anthony. Copyright © 1973 by Michael Anthony. Reprinted by permission of Carlton Publishing Group.

Day of the Butterfly, from DANCE OF THE HAPPY SHADES, by Alice Munro. Copyright © 1968 by Alice Munro. Reprinted by permission of the William Morris Agency, LLC on behalf of the author.

Wolf, extract from "The Angry Winter," in THE UNEXPECTED UNIVERSE, by Loren Eiseley. Copyright © 1968 by Loren Eiseley; renewed 1996 by John A. Eichman III. Reprinted by permission of Houghton Mifflin Harcourt Publishing Company.

ILLUSTRATION CREDITS